AND YET IT MOVES!

OTHER PUBLICATIONS BY DIDIER L. POPPE

ENGLISH

Three men and a dog on a Rock (with Joël
DUFOUR) (Novel) – Xlibris)
Heart to heart from the coach (Sayings) – Xlibris

FRENCH

Trois hommes et un chien sur un Caillou
(avec Joël DUFOUR) – Jets d'Encre
Préavis de brèves (Aphorisms) – Jets d'Encre
En Brèves et contre tout (Aphorisms) – Jets d'Encre
La tête de Cupidon (Theater piece) – Jets d'Encre
Brèves sans trêve (Aphorisms) – Jets d'Encre
Et pourtant il tourne ce monde absurde! (with Joël DUFOUR)
(Short Stories) – Jets d'Encre

WEB SITES

DLPoppe.com (Coach – Writer)
DPTHROWSCOACHING (U Tube) (Coaching)

AND YET IT MOVES!

Short Stories from
Our Absurd World

English Translation by
Didier L. Poppe

To order additional copies of this book, contact:
Xlibris
844-714-8691
www.Xlibris.com
Orders@Xlibris.com
818096

CONTENTS

Acknowledgment

Thank you Joël DUFOUR
Thank you, James THOMAS.

FOREWORD

"That's the Order!"

Our world is absurd, and what's worse is that we don't even notice to what extent. We are doing "the absurd" like Monsieur Jourdain was doing "the prose" (*1) without knowing it. The absurd situation can be compared to when you have missed an exit on the motorway and you have to keep going whether you like it or not on the same road, turning your back to your destination until you find an escape. It is out of the question to go backward and against the traffic!

With the interlacing of situations, logics, and behaviors, one feels like a prisoner of a role-playing game or a motorist stuck on a one-way street.

Absurd dialogues are indeed like impaired talks between normal people. People talk together, but they hear only what they want to hear; it must fit with their own role and the role that they have given from the outset to their interlocutor.

The absurd does not lack logic, like "the fool who has lost everything except his reason" (*2); it is even the triumph of logic over common sense.

The logic is to apply the rule—whatever it is and whatever happens—no matter if the rule is crazy or if it does not fit or cannot be adapted to the situation.

"That's the order!" was the reply the lamplighter gave to the Petit Prince when the latter was wondering about the absurdity of his behavior (*3).

In our world, there are more and more orders and more and more lamplighters, but the Petit Princes, if some are still existing somewhere, have become quite rare.

The absurd can be funny, and it is mostly such when restricted to unusual situations or misunderstandings. This is behind the success of Molière's (*4) comedies and of many comics before and after him.

But this "folie douce" (*5), which makes us laugh, is no longer funny when it turns into furious madness as the characters are unable to find an exit on the motorway and find they are going straight into the no-return point. The laugh changes into a grin, and the grin changes into a rictus.

The comedy becomes a tragedy, and the tragedy becomes a horror!

The bureaucrats of the Nazi horrors were all alleging the administrative logic. They were following instructions, and their files were in perfect order. That was all that mattered to them. In other circumstances, they would have remained perfect lamplighters!

Because the issue with the lamplighters happens when they are employed to do something other than lighting their lamps!

Like the fictional characters from the stories of this book!

Didier L. Poppe

*1. Monsieur Jourdain is the main character from Molière's *Le Bourgeois Gentilhomme* (*The Middle-Class Gentleman*). He discovers that he is talking prose.
*2. G. K. Chesterton, English writer (1874–1936)
*3. *Le petit prince* is the most famous book of Antoine de Saint Exupéry. The little Prince meets the lamplighter, whose duty is to light and shut a lamp every day. Unfortunately, as his planet accelerates its rotation, days turn into hours and then minutes, and the lamplighter is working nonstop.
*4. Molière (Jean Baptiste Poquelin [1622–1673]) is the most famous French comedy writer.
*5. "Sweet madness"

01

Social Care

—Good morning, sir. What can I do for you?

—I would like to get a job.

—Very well. And in what kind of occupation?

—Terrorist!

—Good, but you will first have to fill a file for your application.

—I am already filed.

—Filed?

—Yes, filed S (*1).

—Very well, and do you have already a speciality? Bombs, hostage-taking, car bombs, churches, knives, Kalashnikov, newspapermen assassinations?

—No, not really.

—This is quite unfortunate. It would be easier with a speciality. Do you have any professional experience or references? When did you start working?

—Hmm . . . well, when I was young, I terrorized my cat, and then my parents, and then the house concierge. At school, I terrorized my teachers.

—Yes, this is quite good for an apprenticeship, but then?

—With my buddies, I terrorized the neighborhood, the kids, and also the old ladies. We burned a few cars and extorted money from people.

—This is excellent. Were there any cops inside the cars you burned?

—No!

—Bad luck! That would have given you more points!

—I could not know that.

—Well, do you have any certificates or credential documents?

—Oh yes. I have police-custody records and convictions for assault and theft at gunpoint.

—This should do. Have you been in jail?

—I tried, but they always set me free after my court hearings. They say they don't have enough room. It is not that easy, you know!

—You are not the only one in this situation. Well now, where do you want to work? Go overseas or stay here in France? At the moment, Iraq and Syria are not that interesting. There is nothing left in those places, but in Southeast Asia and Africa, the markets are strong. There are interesting opportunities for young people who are not afraid to expatriate themselves.

—No. I would rather stay here in France. It is safer.

—Did you ever consider starting your own business and being self-employed? You could receive grants and get some advisers to help you.

—No. I don't like people telling me what to do. I don't like advisers, but the grants, I wouldn't mind! You can find me something?

—Yes. You have very interesting records. Here, this is your application. Can you put your signature there? As soon as I get some news, I will contact you. If not, then come back to see me again in two weeks' time.

—And for the grants?

—For the moment, I have filed for you an unemployment-benefit application and a special allowance and a certificate for the mentally disabled. Make sure that you keep this last one as it will serve as an excuse if you start working again. That should do. Goodbye, sir.

—Goodbye, madam. Thank you!

*1. File S is the French police's repertory of potential dangerous people.

02

Fasten Seat Belts

—Stop! Can you pull over on the side of the road, please?

—OK. What is wrong?

—Do you have your driving license with you?

—Yes, here it is. What have I done? I was certainly not driving too fast. You can see that I am a hearse, and our passengers are usually not in a hurry.

—No, you were not speeding, but nevertheless, you are in breach of the security concerning the seat belts.

—What? Why? I have mine on!

—Yes, but your passenger in the back doesn't!

—But he is already dead!

—That doesn't count. The rule says that every passenger in a car—whatever the car—must have their seat belt fastened.

—But he is inside his coffin and as cold as a pint of beer.

—"Beer"? You are right. I can smell alcohol in this car. It stinks! Are you smuggling alcohol in this coffin?

—Certainly not. You can check it if you want. But it could be the products that we use for the preservation of the bodies. I must have spilled some in the process.

—And you think that I am going to believe that story? OK, now you will blow into this tube. And if you are over the limit, we shall detain your

---

car until somebody else comes to drive it, and you will follow us to the police station.

—And leave my customer behind?
—No problem—he can wait here, or you can call a taxi for him.
—But—

—Come on! Blow. Keep blowing. OK, that will do!

03

The Cabin at the Back of the Garden

Dedicated to La Briquette (*1)(*2)

—Now then, what did you learn at school today?

—They talked to us about ecology.

—Ah, and what is that? "Ecology"? Is that some sort of economic housing?

—No, Grandma. You are a bit old-fashioned. Ecology is the science of protecting nature and the resources of the earth.

—Ah, I did not know that we needed a science for that!

—But yes, and there are a lot of very serious people and multiple certificate holders who are experts in this area, and they give us advice. We have to learn how to recycle our waste, and before anything else, we must save water because there are millions of people who don't have drinkable water. Besides that, there are all the problems about hygiene. We are heading for disaster!

—Well, it is not very funny, what you are learning nowadays! You better come with me and take a walk in the garden.

—Say, Grandma, the flowers in your garden are magnificent!

—Yes, they look good for sure—especially at this time of the year.

—But how do you get that? I also grow some flowers, but they are nowhere near as beautiful as yours. Even though I water them and give them a lot of fertilizers and everything!

—All those chemicals? They may not be what they need, no?

—But there are a lot of very serious people and multiple certificate holders who give us expert advice in the gardening magazines. I realize that Grandpa never opens those magazines—even when he goes to the dentist or to the doctor. He prefers the ones with gorgeous girls in swimwear or the princess stories. And in spite of this, he always grows much better vegetables than what you can find at the supermarket.

—Yes, your grandpa indeed does like his father did before him and the father of his father did before him. We did not need this "ecology" and multiple certificated experts. We were doing fine without them, and we respected nature for what it was without trying to change it all the time.

—But you did not even have flush toilets and had no bathroom. That was not hygienic!

—Because you think it is hygienic for people to do their business in clean, drinkable water when half of the world can only get polluted water, if any. Is it ecological to flush all of this down the sewerage drain so that it contaminates the rivers and the sea? This world is getting crazy, and your very serious certificate holders and experts with all their fine speeches will not change anything now. The proof is that, when they have finished their conference, they go and have a piss in good, clean water before catching a taxi to the airport!

—But, Grandma, when you had no bathroom, how did you . . . ?

—Well now, we were going in the cabin at the back of the garden. You see, it is still there. Inside, there is just a plank with a hole, on which you can sit over a pit. Ah, you did not have to be afraid of spiders. They loved the place. And no need for a water flush. Anyways, there was only the water from the well available, and we certainly did not want to spill it. You see, we had to lift the water in buckets with arm strength, and you would not have liked to waste it. These days, many people leave a tap running and don't seem to care!

—But when the pit in the cabin was full, what did you do?

—Then it was a festive day for all the family members who had contributed. First, your grandpa would dig grooves everywhere in the garden. Then he would make some sort of ladle with a perch and a large pot and scoop the stuff out of the hole until it was cleaned out. He poured the mixture into buckets that were carried by the women and the children to be dropped in the grooves. There was a horrible stink in all the village! But the neighbors were mostly giving a hand. That was called a shit party, and we had a lot of fun. When the work was done, we would all go for a swim in the river. The river was not a sewer as it is now, and we had a picnic together on the bank before a game of pétanque or a nap. Those were good times!

—So the secret for the magnificent flowers and the great vegetables, that was it—the cabin at the back of the garden!

—Yes, you see, as your very serious certificate holders and qualified experts—your "ecologists," as they call themselves—when they will have cabins at the backs of their gardens, I shall perhaps start to listen to what they have to say!

*1. La Briquette! A very little house in a very little village in Normandy where my great mother had her cabin at the back of the garden.
*2. In other parts of the world, this might be called a long-drop, outhouse, or privy.

04

Legitimate Offense

—What do you want, Monsieur?

—I would like to register a complaint.

—What sort of complaint? What happened to you?

—I have been attacked!

—What sort of aggression? Sexual, physical, verbal, with a weapon, by a gang?

—Well, um, I have been fired at!

—Ah! This is quite serious. Can you give me more details?

—Well, um, it was last night! At work!

—So you are working night shifts! I suppose that must have happened on your way to or on your way back from work. At these hours, we have many assaults happening in the public transports

—No, it was while I was working.

—A problem with a colleague, then? A quarrel gone wrong? This happens sometimes. Tell me the facts, please.

—No, not a colleague. I was working by myself. I was quietly minding my own business, filling my bag with a few things, when a guy showed up with a hunting rifle in his hands.

—Oh, this seems like it could have been premeditated. Keep going.

—Then he turned on the light, saw me, and shouldered his gun.

—Like that? Straightaway? This makes his case more serious!

—Yes. He just shouted, "You dirty little bastard! I caught you red-handed! Get the fuck outta here, or I am going to put some lead in your ass!"

—So insults and threats—this is the total package! And then what happened?

—Then I ran, dropped my bag, and jumped the fence.

—I understand you. And after that?

—I heard a gunshot, but I was already far away on my motorbike.

—Well! So now you want to file a complaint?

—Yes, and I also want to recover my bag.

—What was in this bag, by the way?

—Well, a bit of everything—electronic gadgets, a few pieces of silver cutlery, a few valuable knickknacks, a phone or two—the usual sort of stuff!

—Ah, you are a secondhand dealer?

—Sort of, but I usually give it to a bro who takes care of that side of things.

—Actually, could you recognize your aggressor?

—No. He was in the dark, but I know where he stays: 21 rue des mimosas.

—Ah, very good, but how did you get his address?

—Well, um, because it was there that all of this happened. Every time, it must have been the owner. That's just my luck. This bastard should have been away on holiday!

—Come on, come on—mind your manners! Well, I am going to receive your complaint. Let me sum this up: aggression with firearm and premeditation, insults, and threats and attempted murder. Is that all?

—No! He also got my bag!

—OK, I had forgotten that. Can you sign the report here? Good. Now you will just have to wait to see how the case unfolds. It can take some time, but don't worry—with a good judge, it should be successful.

—Thank you, Monsieur! Goodbye!

05

God Moves in Mysterious Ways!

—Bless me, Father, because I have sinned.

—Come on, my son. What have you done?

—Well, a lot of things, and I don't even remember some of them.

—Then tell me those that you do know. In his great mercy, the Lord, who sees everything, will forgive you the others if you are repentant.

—Ah, this is great and, at least, quite practical!

—Yes, perhaps, but you have to be sincere in your repentance and determined not to do your sins again. So what have you done, my son?

—Well, one night, I went to the cemetery, and I desecrated some graves.

—What you are telling me is extremely serious. They are the memories of our fathers and mothers that you have profaned. It is a sacrilege!

—Maybe, but for me, my parents are in the sky!

—This is not an excuse or a reason to go after other people's families. Is there anything else?

—Yes. I also painted swastikas in the Jewish cemetery.

—But this is terrible! Do you at least know the meaning of these swastikas?

—No, but I saw in the newspapers that this is what some people do to the Jews.

—But not at all! You have to leave the dead in peace. All the dead deserve respect!

—And for good measure, I also threw a pig's head into the Muslim quarter!

—What a horror! How could you do that? Why so much hatred?

—It was just for fun!

—My son, I feel so sorry for you. Do you realize the consequences of your acts?

—Well . . . no, it is not my fault! In this world, everybody kills everybody else in the name of God. I am bummed to see that, and I told myself, "Wait, I am going to show them how it is disgusting!"

—So you are mad at everybody?

—No, not everybody—just these costumed bastards—the merchants of the temple with their crosses, their crescents, and their stars—the ones who preach for peace and light the wars. Me, if I was God, I would just look after the poor guys who starve to death, and I would not ask to be worshipped for that because I would just be doing my job!

—Yes, but you are not God!

—How would you know?

—Come on, my son. Your anger may be righteous, but even if it does express itself in surprising ways, it cannot be the word of the Lord!

—My son?
—Hey, my son, are you there? Answer me!

—Oh, he has disappeared. I did not hear him go away. He has simply vanished! Come to think of it, I did not see him coming either. I wonder who he could be. Never seen him before. Bizarre!

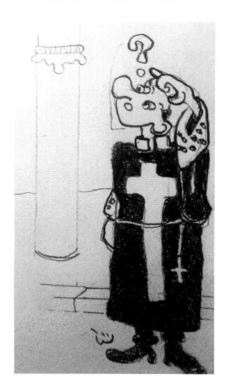

06

Pure Malt

—How's it going? Have you finished setting up the tent?

—Yes. You can already bring our sleeping bags inside, if you want, when you finish starting that campfire.

—It's a nice spot here—near the loch and with the mountains and the forests all around.

—Yes, but there are mosquitoes!

—As there always are near a body of water at this time of the year. But I brought some insect repellent. Here, take the tube.

—Thank you. Thinking of it, it soon should be a good time to pay our respects to this bottle of local product that we bought. These Scottish villages all seem to have their own distilleries and pure-malt brands. Let's try this one. It will help keep us warm.

—Come on! Cheers, Julien!

—Cheers, Christophe!

—He-he, this's good stuff, this one. I do like the smoky aftertaste.

—Yeah, for sure. It has been in a cask for twenty years. Let's have another one!

—By the way, where's Charlie?

—That bloody dog is always busy poking its nose into something. It is as happy as a king here. The country is very wild, and we are away from everything. There must be a lot of rabbits. See? Here he comes now.

—*Bowwow!*

—Look! As I said, Charlie must have caught a rabbit. There is still a tuft of fur hanging from his mouth.

—Yeah, good. Come on. One more glass and then we're off to bed. Nothing better to give us nice dreams!

—OK, let's do it. Bottoms up!

—Bottoms up! And done! Ah, ah!

—Hey, Julien! Wake up!

—Grrmml! Yeah . . . what is it?

—There are bizarre things happening.

—What is this nonsense?

—It's the dog, Charlie. He suddenly got very nervous, jumped up, and ran out.

—He must have heard something—some animal or something—and gone to have a look.

—Yes. I heard him barking and growling not far from our camp.

—I'm sure it's fine. He is just doing his job, guarding us!

—Yes, but after the barking, I heard a big splash.

—Ah, that could have been a fish jumping. The loch is packed with trout and salmon. We should have brought our fishing gear!

—No, it was not a fish. It was much bigger than that!

—Then a dead tree fell. There are a dozen along the shore. The water is eroding the earth under the roots, and this creates submerged caverns. Some are very deep, and who knows what is crawling in there. The tree dies and ends up falling in the lake.

—Yeah, but after the splash, Charlie stopped barking, and he has not come back!

—You . . . you are good at imagining things. Let's call him. Charlie! Charlie! Here, boy!

—You see? No response. Usually, he comes immediately. We should go and have a look!

—OK, if it will reassure you. Let's take our torches and search. You go right. I'll take the left.

—Anything your way?

—Nah, nothing! He has disappeared.

—By golly, this does not seem like him. Wait for the dawn. We shall search more seriously then.

—Don't worry. Tomorrow, he will be here and wagging his tail when we wake up. You'll see.

—Morning, Julien!

—Morning, Christophe!

—And Charlie?

—No sign of Charlie!

—What will we do? We cannot leave things like this and just go away. Let's search again, heading in different directions like last night. Let's meet back here in two hours, OK?

—OK.

—Charlie! Charlie!

—Charlie! Here, boy!

—Nothing?

—Nothing!

—This is nearly incredible. A dog can't simply disappear like that. Something must have happened to it!

—Listen, there is nothing more that we can do here. Best that we go now to the next village and tell the police in case Charlie is found somewhere. We need to start heading home. We have a train to catch.

—OK, let's do just that!

—What did the policeman say? I couldn't understand him.

—He took notes and also proposed a search that will use the police boat to cruise slowly along the shore. That will be faster than by foot, and we can also see better.

—That'll be very helpful. Let's do it and hopefully get to the bottom of this.

—This area is really wild. All these entangled roots and branches, dead trees, reeds—quite difficult to see something. Let's call again.

—Charlie! Charlie!

—Hey, look there! Floating on the water! Something black-and-white!

—It looks like a tuft of fur. Black-and-white, yes!

—And there is some more, trapped in the reeds!

—Shit, do you think it could be Charlie?

—I am afraid so! Oh, this cannot be happening! Poor Charlie! But what could have happened to—

—See the policeman? He has seen the tufts, and he is nodding his head with a bizarre look on his face. Now he is turning the boat around.

—Shit, shit, shit! Charlie, my dog! Poor beast! Charlie!

—Come on. Don't weep, mate. I know what you are feeling.

—Hey, Julien! Wake up!

—Grrmml! Leave me alone. I want to sleep.

—But it is late. The sun is already high in the sky. We have to go. See Charlie? He is impatiently running around!

—*CHARLIE?*

—Yes, Charlie. Why?

—But . . . he's not . . . dead! Dear, I have such a headache. Don't talk so loud!

—Charlie . . . dead? See for yourself. He is jumping all over the place. Now I think that you are having a hell of a hangover. I saw that you finished the rest of the bottle, and you had a very restless sleep. You were talking, shouting, calling Charlie—

—But he had disappeared!

—Oh, no. He was right there all the time—curled up in a ball at our feet. Now get up, go down to the loch, and stick your head into the water to freshen up. Let's get moving! Go! We have quite a way to walk!

—OK, OK, but before anything else, don't talk so loud, please!

—Well, are we ready now, at least? Everything is packed? Can we go?

—Yes, everything is sorted. We can go, but where is that damned dog again? It was there a moment ago.

—Charlie! Hey, Charlie! Here, boy! We are leaving!

—Ah, I can hear him barking over there by the lakeshore—behind those trees—but I cannot quite see him.

—Hey, did you hear that noise? That was a big splash! Like something big was moving in the water!

—Yes, very curious! And Charlie is not barking anymore. Bizarre!

—He must be on his way back to us. He will follow our tracks. Come on, let's go. We have lost enough time. How many kilometers to Inverness (*1)?

*1. Inverness—the closest city to Loch Ness

07

Department of the Demonstrations

Dedicated to the yellow jerseys (*1)

—Good morning, Monsieur. What do you want?

—Good morning. I would like to register a demonstration.

—Very well! Do you already have a date in mind? Have you made a booking?

—Is that so? You have to book?

—Yes, you have to. Nowadays, you know, it is quite busy, and it is safer to book. Everybody wants the same places. Let's see what is available. I assume that you want to demonstrate in the city center?

—Well, yes of course. That is where you are more likely to mess with people. The suburbs are of no use. You need to block some of the main streets, public squares, or administrative buildings.

—Yes, I understand. Please see this. I have an available spot with a major boulevard, a railway station, and a ministry office not far from it— the fifteenth of September all afternoon—would that suit you?

—Which day of the week is that?

—I think it is Thursday.

—Thursday . . . this is not so good. It does break the week. Do you, by any chance, have a Saturday free?

—Saturday? Goodness gracious, it is too much in high demand. You will have to wait until the first of October and then only after 2:00 p.m. Before that, there is already a peace march planned.

—OK. Saturday from 2:00 p.m. to 6:00 p.m.—that will have to do, then!

—Good. Now tell me, how many people are you expecting to march?

—I don't know, really—a thousand, maybe two. It depends on the weather.

—Let's say two thousand. So you fit as a category C demonstration. What sort of people?

—Well, um, a bit of all sorts—students, pensioners, jobless people, workers—

—"Pensioners"? Are you expecting little old ladies?

—Probably, yes, but why?

—They are terrible! They are not aware of anything, and they are very vulnerable. You will have to prevent them from marching at the front and be sure to keep them safe in the middle. No blunders! Are you expecting politicians or personalities?

—I don't know, but it is quite possible.

—Well, as soon as you know, send me a list. No blunders there as well. The usual trick is to put them at the front from the start of the march until the media organizations have taken their pictures. Then, you discreetly move them out of the way before things get rough.

—Very well. I will take your advice on this.

—OK. Now you will also need police and CRS (*2). For a C grade march, I cannot get you more than two squadrons. You will have to make do with them. Where do you want them?

—I think it would be better to place them at the end of the march. It is usually there that the troubles start.

—True, so we shall put them here—at this crossing. Do you anticipate barricades?

—Some people would probably like to build one.

—In that case, you will have to bring your own tires and your own palettes. As a rule, we provide nothing on-site other than the usual pieces of city furniture—park benches, gates, signs, etc.—that are nearby. It might be best for you to bring your materials there on the day before and store them close by. I think that you will want your barricade to be in front of the CRS, so you will have to build it there. OK?

—OK. We shall bring everything we need.

—Concerning the CRS, they will be fitted, of course, with tear gas. Let's say a hundred pieces. That should be sufficient. How many charges do you want them to make?

—Well, I don't really know.

—Let's say two. They are rather overworked at the moment. Are you expecting any excesses?

—"Excesses"?

—Yes—cars set on fire, smashed shop windows, lootings?

—Oh dear, I hope not!

—Of course you don't, but one never knows. So let's say one burned car and one broken shop window to make an estimation. More than that and we will be obliged to severely repress. Of course, you have already briefed the media, newspapers, radio stations, TV channels, and a team of medical volunteers, correct?

—Yes.

—Make sure that they are easy to recognize. No blunders, I remind you! Well now, what should I write in this box—the one for "purpose of the demonstration"?

—It is a demonstration against the demonstrations!

—Come again?

—Yes, we are demonstrating because we are fed up with all these demonstrations. They are spoiling our lives, and we have had enough! What sort of country is this, where everybody is yelling for everything at everybody else? We are the silent majority, and we want our voice to be heard!

—So then, Monsieur, you want to fight fire with fire. It is quite original, but . . . well, everything is OK. Here is your authorization. To summarize, Saturday, October 1, 2:00 p.m. to 6:00 p.m., one major boulevard, two thousand people, old mommies and politicians and personalities under control, two squadrons of CRS with tear gas making two charges, one barricade, and an eventual addition of one burned car and one smashed shop window. Is that right?

—Yes, that's it. Do I have to pay something?

—No, it is free. It's a shame that the government has not thought of introducing a tax on the demonstrations based on the number of participants. That would replenish the state finances!

—But the CRS's hourly salaries, the tear gas, the damages, the cleaning, the municipal furniture, and the repairs?

—Everything is paid for. It is the taxpayer who covers the cost!

—And what if he is not happy to pay?

—Then, he can always organize a demonstration! So au revoir, Monsieur! Have a good day!

*1. Yellow jerseys, people wearing yellow safety jackets, did a number of demonstrations in France in 2018 and 2019.
*2. CRS—French special antidemonstration police unit

08

Constable, You Are Right!

—Stop! Pull over on the side of the street and get off your machine! What is that thing that you are on, by the way?

—It is a bicycle!

—Thank you! I could have guessed that by myself, but I have also noticed that this machine is perfectly irregular: no light at the front, no red light at the back, no mudguards, and before anything else, no brakes! You cannot use this contraption on a public road. This vehicle does not conform with the safety rules.

—Well, um, I did not know.

—So now you do know, and I will give you a ticket, and you must take the necessary changes if you want to use this thing again.

—But, Officer, I cannot modify it. I don't have the right. This is a track bike!

—What do you mean "a track bike"?

—Yes, this is my competition bike. I am a track-cyclist racer—a "pistard [*1]," as they say. And for us, this bike is perfectly normal in the way that it has two wheels, a frame, a handlebar, a saddle, two pedals, and a pair of legs to move the whole thing forward.

—OK, track bike it may be, but what on earth are you doing with it in the middle of the traffic on this boulevard?

—I am going to a competition at the cycling stadium, and because of the traffic jams, I was thinking that I would be faster with my bike than my car. And it's environmentally conscious, no? But I don't want to be late, or I shall lose my title!

    —Ah! So you are a champion?

    —Yes, or at least I was until now. I am a sprint champion.

    —And these things without brakes, they can go fast?

    —Yes. During a sprint, you can reach more than seventy kilometers per hour.

    —That is quite impressive! By the way, do you know that we are in a fifty-kilometer speed zone?

    —Yes, but I assure you that I was going carefully.

    —OK, I will take your word for it. Anyways, here—this is your ticket. Unfortunately, you will have to continue on foot now, pushing your bicycle alongside you. This machine is too dangerous!

    —But, Constable, I will never get there in time to defend my title!

    —I know. Indeed, I said that you will go by foot, but I want you to go to the police car parked there. You will get into it with your bike, and they will take you—

    —To the police station? But I have done nothing wrong!

    —But no! To the velodrome! And I shall even tell the driver to use his lights and siren. Come on, Monsieur! Hurry now!

    —Ah, Officer, how can I thank you?

    —Win the championship and bring your ticket back to me with your autograph at the back! That will be a souvenir for my kid!

    —So you have made the acquaintance of our constable? He is quite strict, and he misses nothing. But all things considered, he is not a bad bloke!

    —Maybe, but he still gave me a ticket.

    —Ah yes? For what reason? Did you read it?

    —No. Wait, I will have a look now. Well . . . oh! I'll be damned!

    —What's wrong?

    —It says on the ticket, "Infraction to be written off in the eventuality of a title"! And here on the back, he has written, "Special authorization for excess speed under special conditions"!

    —You see? Not a bad bloke indeed!

*1. In cycling jargon, *pistards* are the track racers, and *routards* are the road racers. Both words originally come from French.

09

Disciplinary Board

—Good day, Monsieur School Inspector. You wanted to see me?

—Yes. Good day, Monsieur Principal. Please take a seat. So it is about this complaint from Ms. Larue, a teacher in your school—a written complaint that you have forwarded to me through the right channels. It is quite a sensitive issue!

—Yes, indeed, Monsieur School Inspector.

—So if I have understood the matter correctly, this teacher is complaining about two students who she says have published a picture of her underwear in social media. It is alleged that they had made a bet about the color.

—Yes, this is what happened, Monsieur School Inspector.

—According to the teacher, they were sitting in the front row of her class, and several times, they simulated the fall of pens and other objects so they had a reason to go down on all fours under the table. They did this until the teacher got suspicious and discovered that they were surreptitiously operating a mobile phone under the table.

—This is absolutely right, Monsieur School Inspector. The facts are established.

—"Established"? It's you who say that! Did you question the students concerned?

—Yes. They deny any wrongdoing and maintain that they were recovering items that fell from their table and, while doing so, the phone of one of them slipped out of his pocket. And at that very moment, the teacher found them squatting with the phone in their hands.

—It is plausible. But the story with the picture on the social network does not fit this version.

—About that, the students say that it was just a joke and that this picture is a fake that has nothing to do with Ms. Larue's anatomy!

—How can we be sure? The definition of the picture is very poor, and the area was not well lit.

—Yes, we should be given the possibility to compare the picture with the original. But to do this, we would have to ask Ms. Larue to participate in a reenactment so we could get the necessary evidence.

—Monsieur School Inspector, can we really do such a thing? It would be humiliating for this teacher. Her word should be enough for us.

—Yes, certainly. And also, a reenactment would eventually let us discover other contributing factors and see where the responsibility lies.

—How so, Monsieur School Inspector? I don't understand.

—Well, the school furniture, to start with. Was the teacher's desk open or closed at the front? Obviously, it was open because the students could see her legs. And also, how high was the platform that the teacher's desk was on? Was it of a height that encouraged teenagers to have this sort of idea? Then at what distance was the first row of student tables from the teacher's desk? Are there any official instructions on these points? All these factors could be considered as attenuating circumstances. It will certainly not look good for us and more especially for YOU, the principal of this institution, if these factors become known and used. Do not forget that, as the head of this school, you may well be held partly responsible.

—Oh, I see, Monsieur School Inspector. This is clearly not desirable. So what can we do? I have called for a disciplinary board next Thursday!

—Don't continue with that! Without proof, we cannot condemn these two rascals. I can already imagine their parents invading my office, demonstrating in the street, or complaining to the media. All we need now is for these people to belong to some ethnic or religious group, and the Ministry of Education, which I am representing, doesn't want such troubles. Do I need to paint you a picture of the situation?

—I understand this quite well, Monsieur School Inspector. But what are your instructions? This is now well outside my area of competence, and I certainly don't want to undermine the reputation of our administration.

—Concerning the two students, you will forbid them from sitting at the first row and ban them from carrying a phone inside the school's limits. But as we must not forget the educational aspect of this situation and meet their possible aspirations, you will also encourage them to join the photography club of the school and aspire to their potential. I will leave you free to orally reprimand them, but not a word must go out of your office!

—And what about the teacher?

—You will take the necessary measures to adjust the school furniture in your establishment. In fact, concerning this point, I am thinking about writing a report to the ministry to ask for new guidelines on a national scale. In addition, you will summon this teaching colleague to your office to remind her that our careers comprise sacrifices and compromises. So It would be preferable for the good name of our service that from now on, she wears trousers. If there is a problem, you can always move her to another class. There are not enough facts at the moment to justify moving her to a different school. To facilitate these things, you will be also entitled to confidentially inform her that I shall look for a way to give her a helping hand with her next career advancement. Do you see anything else, Monsieur Principal?

—No, Monsieur School Inspector. No blunders and no questions asked. It is better for everybody!

—Very well, Monsieur Principal. I will not take up any more of your time. I have other issues waiting for me.

—I can imagine, Monsieur School Inspector. Please accept my thanks and appreciation.

—Thank you, Monsieur Principal. I wish you a pleasant day.

—Ah, wait a moment. I nearly forgot something. About your application for the Academic Palms Award (*1), don't forget to send it to me as soon as possible through the normal channels. I have good reason to believe that it is going to be favorably received!

—Ah, Monsieur School Inspector, you overwhelm me! How can I thank you?

—There's no need! Just keep doing a great job as a principal. Is not the education of our young people our common interest and burden?

*1. Academic Palms is a French award for the world of culture and education. It has three levels: knight, officer, and commander. Foreign recipients can also be nominated.

10

Fracture on the Headline

—Good. Is everybody here? Yes? We can start, then. I am waiting for your suggestions about the articles that we will include in our next edition. This week, there haven't been a lot of newsworthy happenings that will grab the public's attention, and I have the feeling that we will have to rehash or refresh some old go-everywhere subjects. John, tell me what we have got.

—Boss, we do have a few possibilities from the dispatches. There is a new shipwreck of migrants in the Mediterranean. Maybe about fifty drowned. There was also a typhoon in Asia, and they are talking about seven hundred casualties!

—Well, but all of this is not very new. It has become routine. People are overfed with this sort of information, and they don't react anymore. What else, then?

—There is a soccer player in the national team who injured himself while training.

—Ah! Who? And what sort of injury?

—Baston! He twisted his ankle, but the medical people are still investigating.

—Oh! This is serious. Will he be able to play against Germany in two weeks? People will be anxious to know, and we have to give them the information they need. Come on! I want a picture of the guy with his bandaged foot, interviews with the coach and the medical staff, and the reactions of some supporters.

—But, Boss, *L'Equipe* (*1) will already have covered the matter and made a fuss about it. We should not look like we are copying them. We are an information journal, not a sports paper.

—True, but when one has nothing more serious, sports news come in very handy. OK, if you want, we won't make it our headline, but we will still put the info teaser in the front page and the full article with pictures in our sports pages.

—And what are we doing with the migrants and the Asians?

—The migrants, you put them in page 2. Make a small text box of about twenty lines with the usual controversy about the people traffickers, the NGOs, etc. The typhoon in Asia? We don't have many details at the moment, and it's a long way from here! Write three to four lines in the diverse international news section.

—OK, Boss. We are on it.

—Well, guys, back now to the Une (*2). We need to find something that really hooks our readers. Let's make a roundup of the possibilities. International politics?

—Nah, it's been the usual brinkmanship and posturing: some more or less bullshit conferences, some more or less crooked politician encounters, some more or less forced commercial treaties, and some more or less manipulated armed rebellions. Everybody is interfering with everybody else's affairs. We can always write a filler article with pictures of guys shaking hands or going out of their cars, if we need to.

—Very well! Prepare something in case we don't have anything better. National politics?

—Pretty much the same, Boss—no real surprises. Our zealous elected officials are quite busy squabbling or knifing one another in the back, especially when two belong to the same party.

—Is there not a minister who has recently said or done some shitty thing that we could turn into a big issue? That's what they are good for, no? A good little scandal from behind the bundles that we reveal to the public—that would boost our circulation. The good people that we write for will be furious to see how their tax money is wasted and need to vent their anger on some scapegoats!

—OK, Boss! We'll scan the social media sites to find something. Anyways, the thing is that politics is done on Facebook, Instagram, or Twitter and not in the House of Representatives!

—And it might be good to throw in a bit of fake news to give the anthill a kick. We would surely get some interesting reactions from this smart set of people who get indignant so easily!

—Yes, but we don't want anyone to trace it back to us. We'll have to discreetly go through a third party.

—This is not really a problem. We have the connections for that!

—Sounds good, but what sort of item?

—We are not short of choice: financial embezzlements, electoral scams, sex scandals, appointment gravy trains, nepotism, monstrous restaurant or tailor bills, etc. OK, you search for something and get back to me as soon as possible.

—Very well, Boss. We shall begin immediately.

—Yes, but this still does not give us a good headline! We have to investigate other things: the holidays, the pollution, the police brutality, the fuel prices, the globalization, the taxes, the bureaucrats, the terrorism, the global warming, the insecurity, the drought, the suburban problems, the feminists, the jail scandal, the nuclear threat, the mess that's our educational system, the royal family—come on! Move your asses! I need at least a dozen articles ready on my desk before three o'clock, and then we will use the best one to make the headline.

—OK, Boss! Understood!

—And be sure to take care about what you are writing. Don't forget the political angle of our publication. We are writing news—that's right—but we pick the news that suits us. I don't need to remind you who owns the paper and is paying you! Ah, wait a second. What is it, Sylvain?

—Boss, there is a dispatch that has just come through!

—And? You look a bit peculiar! What happened?

—It is Baston, Boss. The results of his x-ray scan.

—So what is it?

—It is a fracture, Boss. He will not be able to play! It is a catastrophe!

—Have you finished the layout of the Une?

—Yes, Boss. It's done.

—Let me see. "France, who will pay for the fractures?" He-he, quite clever! And it sounds good! And I like the picture of the guy going out of the hospital with his crutches. Now, concerning the article, make sure that it will draw a parallel between the footballer's fracture, the social fractures of the country, and the "factures [*3]" for the damages done by the demonstrations. I hope that you wrote it the way I wanted. Very good! Now we can proceed to the printing!

*1. *L'Equipe* is a French daily sports newspaper.
*2. The Une is the first page of a newspaper and has all the headlines.
*3. Intentional relation between *fracture* (fracture) and *facture* (bill).

11

Please, Draw Me an Idiot! (*1)

A tribute to Antoine de Saint Exupéry

The ship was progressing laboriously and close-hauled as possible. The sea was still choppy after the last storm had gone, and each wave was inflicting a shock that made the hull and the sails vibrate. I had virtually not slept in three days, having to stay at the helm to keep my course. I could have chosen an easier way, but in a solitary sailing race, you must not go for the comfort and you have to calculate the risks.

From time to time, I would doze off, but then I would be woken with a start by a wave bigger than the others, and I would give an instinctive pull on the bar to prevent the ship from being rolled over by the swell.

Clinging to the helm, I must have lost consciousness a bit longer than usual when I was suddenly woken by the sound of a voice: "Hello? Ho! Ho! Do you hear me?"

I hastily opened my salt-burned eyes; it was like brutally waking up from a dream.

"Well, hey! If you could see your face! You were sleeping soundly!"

No matter how hard I shake my head and blink my eyes to make the mirage disappear, there was still in front of me a young boy—sitting in the cockpit and looking at me while smiling!

"But . . . but . . . you, what are you doing here? How did you get here?"

We were a thousand miles away from the nearest inhabited country!

"Me? Well, I was just wandering in the sky, and I saw your boat—all alone in the middle of the ocean. Then I told myself that you would probably need some company. It is not good to stay alone!"

"Now wait! You were wandering in the sky? As simple as that?"

"Yes, on a falling star. From time to time, I leave my planet and go for a little trip. You know, I have already been on this planet. It was a long time ago. I landed in a desert that time. It was very hot. By luck, there was somebody like you, but he had a plane, not a ship."

I looked at him more carefully. He could be six to eight years old, not more, with fair hair and a child's face but with serious blue eyes. He wore a baseball cap on his head and light-blue overalls with a sailor-striped jersey and a pair of small red rubber boots.

"Ah! I believe I can guess who you are. You know, the guy with the plane, he told the story of your encounter in a book—a nice book with drawings and such a great lesson: 'The essential can only be seen with the heart!'"

"This is true. I remember now. I would like to have this book. Do you have it here?"

"Alas, no. When I am racing, I only take the bare minimum. No useless weight!"

"Because a book is a useless weight? It is like a friend, no?"

"Yes—in fact, no. You are disturbing me a bit with your questions."

"And the guy with the plane, do you know him? Where is he now?"

"Unfortunately, he is dead. His plane crashed into the sea. It was because of the war!"

I regretted telling the truth because he immediately dissolved into tears.

"War! I hate war! Only mankind does war. They are too stupid and mean. And you, you are also making war with your ship?"

"No. I am racing. It is called sport. It is a bit like war because you aim to win, but you are not killing people. Come on, don't weep!"

He dried his eyes, and while still snuffling, he said, "I prefer that. I don't want you to do war."

"You know, many people are idiots. One fills their heads with rubbish, and soon they find themselves at war without even wanting it."

"'Idiots,' you say? This is a curious word! Please, can you draw me an idiot so that I can recognize them?"

"You know, I am not very good at drawing, and I have to look after my boat."

"This is not a problem. I shall take the helm while you are drawing."

The weather and the sea had been improving, and I decided to take the risk. I searched for a piece of paper and a pen inside the boat. As best as I could, I drew an operetta soldier who was marching the goose step with a gun on his shoulder and a bearskin.

"Here—this is an idiot soldier. There are many like him, you know!"

He looked at the drawing and pouted.

"No, I don't want an idiot soldier. It will remind me too much of the war and my friend, the aviator. Draw me something else!"

I drew a guy on his knees, prostrating himself.

"Here—this one is a religious idiot. There are many like him too. They believe in anything, and they want other people to be like them. Otherwise, they kill and lay bombs."

"No, I don't want this one either. Why should you force others to share your beliefs? Draw me something less sinister. Are there not idiots who are less nasty?"

"Yes, there are those who are called brave idiots. Indeed, they are the most common!"

"Yes, that's it! Please draw me a brave idiot!"

I took a moment to think. How to draw a brave idiot? That was far beyond my artistic capacities! He was starting to get a bit on my nerves with his mania about drawings. As a last resort, I drew a sky with a star in a corner and then the sea with waves forming white crests, and on the sea, I drew a ship with sails that was a bit like mine.

"Here. You see the sky? Here is your star. Under it, you can see the sea. There is my ship, and inside the ship, there is a brave idiot. It's me!"

"This is it! It is exactly the way I wanted it!"

12

The Referee to the John!

—Good morning, Mr. League President. You wanted to see me?

—Good morning, Mr. Club President! Yes. Thank you for coming. I believe that we have a few points to settle after what happened at your home ground last weekend.

—What happened?

—It's about the soccer match between your team, La Petite Ferté, and the one from Sainte Guduche. According to the report I have received from the referee, Monsieur Lecrampon, there were some regrettable incidents— brawls, invading of the field, and insults, to name but a few.

—Oh, it is just about that? Nothing really to make a fuss about! In fact, it was just like the previous years. At our annual derby, it is always a bit animated, for sure!

—Yes, but this year, you were required to have an official referee, and Monsieur Lecrampon was assigned. He related that he was insulted by the spectators and told that he had better go to the toilets by people singing, "The referee to the John! The referee to the John!" Is that right?

—Yes, but no harm was intended. It was just to give a folkloric atmosphere to the game. To say the truth, we don't even have public toilets at the place!

—What? No toilet? But how do people—and I'm not even mentioning the referees!

—No problem—the men go to the bush behind the buvette (*1)!

—But the ladies?

—In the case of an emergency, they can go to Old Dad Francis's cabin, which is at the back of his garden. The playing field belongs to him, and he lets the club use it as it happens to be the flattest field of the village.

—You don't have a real soccer field?

—No. Why should we have one? We are not going to waste good fertile ground so that a bunch of guys can kick a leather ball around from time to time. Anyways, we don't have stands either, if you want to know everything.

—Well, it's peculiar. Let us assume that! But there have been several fights between the players and also between the spectators!

—Yes, but what else can you expect? People are coming just for that. You cannot stop them from having their fun. I assure you that it is all without bad intentions—just some little rivalries and old accounts to settle. This makes them really good friends!

—Indeed, you have a curious way of presenting the facts. Besides, I notice that you are displaying a rather black and swollen eye!

—Sure. It was the beadle from Sainte Guduche. He is the president of their sports club. Quite a solid fellow, one has to admit, and one who can punch hard. But I gave him a run for his money, and he must have a painful jaw at the moment! Of course, we had a drink together to celebrate after the game.

—But to fight, you need to have a good reason. I don't know—a disallowed goal, a tackle too rough?

—No, nobody cares about the game! It is just traditional between our two neighboring villages. At Sainte Guduche, they are more clergy-oriented, and we, at the Petite Ferté, are strongly for the left. This annual match is a good opportunity for us to meet again. The young fellows, they have the soccer, and we, the older ones, get a bit of exercise to stay fit!

—Bravo! What a great attitude indeed! If everybody was doing it like you, it would not be good for our sport!

—But you know that one can see a lot more happening on TV—with the hooligan brawls, the smashed shop windows, and worse. We, at least, have the right sporting spirit. When the game is finished, we have a barbecue and a few drinks together. The Sainte Guduches, they bring a sheep, and we get a pig. And when we have all our bellies filled, everyone goes back home with the feeling that he has done his duty!

—It is hard to believe what you are telling me, and I understand now that Monsieur Lecrampon was a bit overtaken by the events.

—Yes. When one only knows about the rules, he still has a lot to learn about how to manage people. Next time, he will know better and will adapt to the situation.

—Unfortunately, Monsieur President of La Petite Ferté, I am afraid that Monsieur Lecrampon will not be assigned to your local derby again.

—Why is that? We need an official referee. It looks more serious for the people.

—Don't be afraid! You need an official, and you will get one, I promise you.

—Ah, thank you! And who are you thinking to send next time?

—Well, I am planning to come myself!

—YOU? Mr. League President, this is an honor! But why?

—Well, my friend, believe it or not, I would also like to have some fun myself. Vive (*2) the return to the roots! And I do hope that the sheep and the pig will be there again and properly roasted!

*1. *buvette*—an open-air bar
*2. *Vive*—"Long live" in French

13

Vocational Test

—Good morning, sir! Are you looking for some information?

—Yes, thank you. I would like to know what I need to do to enter the police force.

—The police force? But which section?

—Ah, there are several?

—Yes, depending on the specialities. You have the local city police, the national police, the border police, the GIGN (*1), the criminal police, the port police, the transport police, the vice police, and a few more!

—So many! That's a lot of people. With all of these, the criminals will have to behave! Would it be easy to find me a place, then?

—This is not so easy. First, because these positions are in high demand and also because you need to have the right qualifications, pass the entrance examination, and go to a training school before you can obtain a position. But before anything else, you need to get through a preliminary test that will help us get you on the right path. Don't be afraid. It is a test that will show how you deal with situations. It is not very long, and the questions are multiple-choice.

—And where can I sit this test?

—Here, and you can do so now, if you want. I can give you the questionnaire, and you can sit right there and complete the test. You will have half an hour. Are you ready?

—Yes. Bring it on.

—Here it is. You can start now. Good luck!

—Well, let's see this questionnaire. Dear, it's quite long, and it's written small. Good, it says, "Tick the right answer." Easy!

Question 1: You are going for your daily jog when, in front of you, an old lady has her bag snatched by a malefactor.

   A) You run after the malefactor and try to arrest him.
   B) You pretend to see nothing and keep running.
   C) You run to help the old lady.

—Well, um, if I run after the malefactor, I am not sure that I can catch him. If I try to help the old lady, I don't know what I am going to do with her. Then I'll pick answer B. There is no doubt about it!

Question 2: During a demonstration, a protestor insults you.

   A) You pretend not to have understood.
   B) You answer by insulting him back.
   C) You complain to your chief.

—This one is quite difficult. I cannot decide between A and C. Let's go with C because in case of doubt, one must always refer to the hierarchy.

Question 3: An old chap tries to cross the road when the light for pedestrians is red.

   A) You stop the traffic and help the old fellow cross the road.
   B) You let him go and cross your fingers, hoping nothing will happen to him.
   C) You call 111 and the emergency rescue in anticipation of an accident.

—No problem with this one. I'll pick C because of the precautionary principle.

Question 4: You stop a speeding female driver. (You can pick several right answers.)

   A) You immobilize her vehicle and offer to take her back home.
   B) You get ready to offer your handkerchief if she starts weeping.
   C) You pretend that you have lost your pen and cannot write the ticket and let her go with only a warning.

—Well, um, it depends on how good-looking she is. The easiest is B, but you need to have a clean handkerchief, or it will be embarrassing!

Question 5: You are on night duty and are guarding an apartment where a well-known personality is making a very private visit. In the morning, he asks you to buy some coffee and croissants.

A) *You buy two more croissants and a coffee for yourself.*
B) *You buy the stuff, come back, and enter the apartment without knocking.*
C) *You ask for reinforcements so that you can leave your post and do the job.*

—The whole night! It's quite long! I think I would deserve A, but if I was in this situation, it would be fun to do B and look at their faces when I walk in. Hah!"

Question 6: A guy is shooting with a gun at night in a hot suburb.

A) *You give him a ticket for disturbing the peace at night.*
B) *You wait until he has used all his ammunition.*
C) *You call the police.*

—Ah, one has to be cautious. I would rather call the police and let my colleagues deal with the problem. What? I am one of the police, yes, but I cannot do everything anyway!

Question 7: You have to conduct an inquiry in a nudist camp.

A) *You call them and ask them to put their clothes on before intervening.*
B) *You take off your uniform and enter the place incognito.*
C) *You ask them to show their papers.*

—One has to always check the IDs of people before you start interviewing. So this is easy. It's C.

Question 8: When can you use your service revolver?

A) *When you have it in your hand*
B) *When you have given the customary warnings*
C) *When you have time to use it*

—Of course I shall tick A! How can you use your gun if you don't have it in your hand? These questions are stupid!

—Good sir, have you finished with the questionnaire? Give it to me, please. Thank you. Let's have a look. I will be able to tell you soon if you have succeeded. I see that you picked B, C, C, C, B, C, and A.
—Is that OK?

—Well, Monsieur, this is excellent! You seem to have the necessary thinking capacity to deal with delicate situations. So I shall now give you a summons for the entrance examination, and you will only have to choose your speciality.
—Oh, I have already made my mind up on that.
—Ah, good. Can I know which one?
—What about the police of the police? It would suit me like a glove!

*1. GIGN is a special French police corps.

14

O Ral, O Despair!

—OK, young man, it is your turn. What is the question that you have drawn for your verbal examination? Let me see . . . ah! "The French Revolution and the first empire." Very good! A vast subject! You can start.

—Well . . . then . . . the revolution, it is when people revolted . . .

—Quite an evidence! But expand that idea. Who revolted? Against whom? And why?

—Ah, they revolted because they were not happy.

—I could guess that, but what were the causes of this resentment? Can you name some?

—Well . . . because they had no money!

—Of course, that's generally the case, but was that all?

—So . . . they could not buy food or go to the restaurants!

—Yes, I see. I am going to help you a bit. Did you hear about July 14 (*1)?

—Well, yes. There is the firework show, people dancing in the street, and the parade on the Champs Elysées.

—Yes, but why just on July 14? Is there any relation with the French Revolution?

—Ah yes, I remember now. It is the day they took the pastille (*2)!

—The "pastille"? Are you not confusing it with the Bastille? It's not a contraceptive pill!

—Ah . . . so what? Pastille, Bastille, Pill—it's all the same, no?

46

—I shall try to help you again. Do you know about *république* and *nation*?

—Yes—these, I know. These are metro stations!

—Besides that, the word *république* does not mean anything to you? Did we always have a republic?

—No. Before, we had a king!

—Here we have something, at least! And was there a king when the revolution started?

—Probably . . . yes, it was the king of France!

—Here, we have something, at least! Well, that makes some sense, by any chance, would you know the name of this king?

—Wait, I am searching . . . Pelé? No, that is a soccer king. So . . . ah! I know that they had numbers!

—Good, and if I give you the name, could you give me the "number," as you say? So it was Louis, but Louis how much?

—I don't know. Maybe V or VI? There were at least a dozen of them, I believe!

—Bad luck—it was Louis XVI, and what do you know about the first empire?

—Ah, this I know. It was Louis the Funeste (*3).

—You want to say Louis de Funès, I suppose. I am afraid that there is confusion in your mind! And what about Napoléon? Does that name awaken anything in you?

—Yes, yes. I have seen the movie. He was the one who replaced the king. And he also had a number!

—Here, you surprise me, and which number?

—Well . . . XVII, no? Because they were already at XVI!

—I admire your logic. What a pity that it is not supported by some knowledge! You would certainly benefit from making some more friendship with some of the personalities of your country's history.

—Friends? I've got plenty of them on Facebook, but Napoleon and Louis XVI, they did not send me any friend request. So how could I know about them?

—Effectively, I understand it is their fault! Well, thank you for coming. That will be enough. You can move to the other juries to complete your oral exam. Good luck!

—So, my dear colleague, what do you think about that?

—Alas, like you, I am afraid. We had to deal with a perfect ignorant, if not a perfect dummy, who will become a perfect elector, if not a perfect citizen!

—Nevertheless, we have to give him a score. I remind you that with the new regulations, every mark under 5 must be justified by a report.

—Sod the reports!

—Anyways, they will lift all the marks to get to the official percentage of passes needed for this exam. How much is it now? 92 percent? 95 percent? What a shame!

—Besides that, if you, as an examiner, give too many bad marks, then next year, they don't take you again, and you will lose your examiner's fees!

—Yes, we are paid to clown around, so let's be clowns!

—That being said, my dear colleague, one cannot completely blame that young man. If we had questioned him about the characteristics and programs of this or that computer, he would perhaps teach us something, and it would be we who looked like idiots.

—Yes, I see what you mean, but it's him who is taking an exam, not you and me!

—Then, if you agree, how about we give him a 6 out of 20 and he can hang somewhere else? With the official adjustments, it will be lifted to 8, and they will probably get that low to "save" more candidates, so it is nearly impossible to fail now. Anyways, it will be up to the universities to deal with the baby!

—Yes, unless somebody one day has enough courage and common sense to stop this circus!

—Hey! How did you do? What question did you get?

—Oh dear, it was quite difficult! Something about the revolution, the metro stations, and the pastille.

—Wow! And what did you tell them?

—A lot of stuff: the Fourteenth of July, the kings of France, Napoléon XVII . . .

—Well, I did not expect you to know so much. You will get a high mark, you lucky bastard!

Can you help me a little? Just in case I get the same question!

*1. The Fourteenth of July is the national day of France.

*2. It celebrates the taking of the Bastille, a fortified prison in Paris. There is a voluntary confusion between *Bastille* and *pastille* as *pastille* can also be understood to be the contraceptive pill.

*3. Louis de Funès is one of the most famous French comic-movie actors. There is a voluntary confusion between his name, *Funès*, and *funeste*, which means "evil or disastrous."

15

Local Products

—Ah, good morning, Monsieur. I am happy to meet you.
—Good morning. Why?
—You are the mayor of this village, I believe?
—This is right!
—Then I would like to make some observations.
—You are welcome to do so. I am listening.

—Thank you. We have recently moved to your village. It is us who bought the old barn near the entrance of the village and have transformed it into a nice country house. We moved in just one month ago.
—Yes, La Coudraie (*1). I know the place. Years ago, it was a little farm.
—Perhaps, but when we bought it, it was more or less in ruins. We have restored and transformed it. We came every weekend and during the holidays, but now we are going to live there permanently. We named it Country Home (*2).
—Ah! You think it sounds better than La Coudraie? Anyways, it is your choice. I hope you are doing well there. You were living in the city before, I guess?
—Yes, I am working as a councillor for the development of the mobile infrastructure in the department of personnel of the decentralized services of the Ministry of the Environmental Transition and Equity!

—Dear, that's quite a name! You need to have some breath and memory to get it right! Never heard of it myself, but I suppose that it's not about that, that you want to talk. The life in the country must be quite a change for you.

—Yes, but it hasn't exactly been what we were expecting. It is not as peaceful as it looks. In fact, it is very noisy!

—Noisy?

—Yes! First, there is the church with its bloody bells ringing every quarter hour, and then it breaks loose at every full hour and has a double package at midday.

—Yes, but the pastor stops it at night. We have an agreement about that.

—Yes, that's something, but even so, it starts at seven o'clock in the morning—even on Sundays. And that's the end of your weekend chance for late sleeping.

—Well, yes, but here, nobody sleeps late. On Sundays, people go to the early mass as they have their cows to milk. Besides that, it is the church's carillon that marks the life of the village. People rely on those bells and on the sun to know the time. Most of them don't even carry watches.

—If it was only that, that would be OK, but at five o'clock in the morning, the bloody rooster on the neighbor's farm starts vocalizing, and it keeps going for a good fifteen minutes. It finds nothing better to do than perching itself in a tree just over our bedroom window. One of these days, I am going to shoot it!

—Oh dear, don't do that! I know your neighbor, and that would be like a declaration of war. And if I remember correctly, this tree that you are referring to is on his property.

—Yes, but the branches are over ours, and they are just the ones where that damned beast chooses to post itself!

—Well, in the end, this cock crow does not last too long!

—Yes, but the point is that it does wake up everybody as well as the animals. The cows of this same neighbor start to get moving, all by themselves, and head off for milking. Not only do we hear the mooing, but there are some who carry a bell, and the dog barks after them. It is a cacophony!

—Bof! You'll see that you will get used to it. Surely this is better than the picking up of the garbage cans in the city, no?

—Maybe, but that is not all. When the milking is done, the farmer loads the cans of milk in his trailer. It seems that he is enjoying himself while banging them! A racket that gets even worse when he starts his tractor!

—Yes, but he has to deliver his milk early. People are waiting for it!

—And when he comes back half an hour later, all the empty cans are bumping around. It's even worse.

—Yes, but after that, it gets quieter, no? When everybody has gone to work in the fields, there is nobody left at the farm, and you can go back to sleep.

—You've got to be kidding me! There are all the cows passing on the path in front of our house on their way to their pasture. They seem to be competing to see who can moo the loudest and the longest. And to finish the picture, once they have gone by, the road is covered with fresh dung, and it really smells!

—The country air is certainly invigorating, for sure! It is quite a change when you have been raised with car-exhaust fumes.

—And in the evening, when they come back, it happens all over again, and we are good for a second layer. Could they not clean up after their cows? In the city, when you walk your dog, you have to pick up its droppings, or you get a fine!

—Ah, in the city? Let's talk about the city! You have the demonstrations, and those make a lot of noise. They break everything, and you have to clean and pay for the damages. Here, at least, a good rain does the job for free. If you ask our municipal council to introduce such a rule, you will have some deaths on your hands. All these old fellows have spent their whole lives behind the asses of their cows, and they will die while laughing at the idea!

—Well, actually, it's not just the cows! The other day, the farmer found nothing better to do than spread liquid manure on his field—just behind our place. For one week, it stank horribly, especially when the wind blew toward our windows. It was so bad that we had to cancel some friends' invitations.

—It is unfortunate, indeed, but he has to fertilize his fields before planting his potatoes. And what's more, it is a natural fertilizer—no chemicals! The ecology is to spread the shit in the fields, not to start it in the street! Are those all your complaints?

—No, there are also the ducks. They saw that we had built a swimming pool and must think that it is for them, and now they swim in it!

—Quite funny, no?

—That would be the case if they were not shitting all over the place!

—Sure, these ducks are difficult to educate when they have it in mind to take a swim. You could use a scarecrow or a net?

—Well, maybe. There is also the issue that we are finding the village is a little dead. No MacDo, no kebab, no Chinese restaurant—there is only a bistro (*3), a butcher, a bakery, and just one dairy!

—You know, Monsieur, we have survived like this for centuries, and we have in mind to keep things as they are—with our local products. You, a true Frenchman, are you not fond of a good steak frites, a jambon-beurre sandwich, a potée aux choux, or some confit de canard (*4)? Or do you prefer junk food?

—Yes, of course I love our traditional cuisines. I must admit that in the cities, you can easily get bad eating habits. People are lazy. Yes, the good products of the country do taste much better and are healthier.

—So you see! These good products—they are just here, wandering under your windows, waking you up early in the morning, and perfuming your air. They are surely worth some sacrifices or some concessions. By the way, do you know about Monsieur Alphonse Allais?

—Yes. He was a humorist, I believe.

—Yes, and a Norman humorist. He was a guy from around these parts, and we are proud of that. Now our Monsieur Allais, back in his day, wrote, "One should better build the cities in the country!"

—Yes, yes, I remember hearing that. So it is he who said that?

—Yes, but now, if he was still living, I believe he would change his quote and say, "It should be better to build the country houses in the cities!"

—Ah, Monsieur Mayor, you are a funny man, but don't worry—I understood the lesson.

—Bof! It was not meant to be a lesson—just my own observation. You see, here we may be shitkickers, but we still have some culture. I wish you a good day, Monsieur.

—Have a good day yourself, Monsieur Mayor!

*1. *La Coudraie* is the French name for a thicket of hazelnut trees

*2. "Country Home" was written in English in the original text. French snobs like to use English words.

*3. *Bistrot* (bistro) is the name for a small café where commoners like to have a drink and socialize.

*4. Steak frites (steak and french fries), jambon-beurre sandwich (bread baguette with ham and butter), potée aux choux (cabbage hotpot), and confit de canard (duck confit) are unmissable specialities of France's food culture.

16

It's a Sign!

Dedicated to Nils, an MMA fighter

—Come on, boy. Sit there. Breathe deeply. Give me your hands so that I can lace your gloves. Here, the left one first, if you want. Are you OK?

—Yes, I'm fine, Monsieur Gonzales. It's just a bit hot here.

—Look! Here, have a drink of this. It will refresh you. But don't swallow. Spit it out in the basin. So this hand is done. Give me your right one now.

—Monsieur Gonzales, the other guy at the opposite corner, he does not stop moving!

—It's a sign, boy! He is afraid, and that will make him nervous. Don't let yourself be impressed. He just likes to be showy.

—Now it's about to start. The referee is calling us to the center of the ring.

—Don't worry, it is just for the standard instructions. Go now!

—It's as you said, Monsieur Gonzales. He told us everything that you already explained to me.

—Good. Quick! Before the bell sounds, remember your tactic for the first round. Keep your distance. Let him come. Content yourself with countering and hitting back. Toward the end of the round, try for a sequence or two to see how he is reacting, and if he uses the same dodges, go for it! Ah, the bell! Come on, boy!

—OK, Monsieur Gonzales. Keep my distance. I have understood.

—Well, quick! Sit down, boy! Breathe deeply! Here is the towel. Well, it was not too bad. You controlled him. He is the nervous type for sure, and he moves a lot.

—Yes, but it was hard to get a clear shot while keeping my distance. He is fast. He had a left that I did not see coming, and it landed on my cheekbone. I hit him in the body, but it did not seem to trouble him.

—This is normal at the beginning of a fight. Just keep going. It is good to score points. Now, if he is faster than you, you will have to look for a hand-to-hand fight. See if you can push him against the ropes and trap him there. If he refuses the close fight, it's a sign!

—That's good, Monsieur Gonzales. Hand-to-hand, close fighting—I have understood!

—The bell! Boy, here you go now!

—Ooh la la, he got me. I nearly hit the floor. He is punching hard, this bastard!

—Breathe, breathe. Calm down. Here, a bit of icy wet sponge to clear your mind. This is nothing. Breathe!

—But what should I do now, Monsieur Gonzales? The hand-to-hand stuff, it did not work. He got me when I tried to move closer.

—Listen, boy: These nervous guys, they don't last more than two or three rounds. You have to get them out of breath, and when they start to get tired, *baboum*—you nail them. Close your guard, block everything, pretend to attack from time to time, and make him move. If he always dodges, that's a good sign!

—That's good, Monsieur Gonzales. Sure, I'll make him move. I have understood.

—The bell! Come on, boy! It's your round!

—Quick, boy! Here is your stool. Hold yourself steady with the ropes and sit. Spread your legs. Wait, I am going to treat your cut.

—Ah, Monsieur Gonzales, is it bad? I have blood running into my eye.

—No, it is not so bad—just a little cut on the eyebrow. With the cream, it will stop. Now listen. You have to protect yourself better than that. Get your guard a bit higher. Don't let him hit you in the same spot. He will try to, but knowing that, it will be a good opportunity for you to score a counterpunch. Look, he is starting to slow down his tempo. They are making him breathe and are massaging his legs. It's a sign!

—That's good, Monsieur Gonzales. I shall play the counterattack. I have understood.

—The bell? Already? Come on, boy! Hang tough!

—Hey, boy! This way! You were going to the wrong corner. Sit there and show me your eyes. This one is a bit swollen, and the other one is also cut. But what on earth were you doing out there? You cannot stand there like that and let him bombard you without doing anything!

—But, Monsieur Gonzales, you told me to play the counterattack. To do that, you have to let the other attack, no?

—Yes, but not like that. You have to counter. That means that you have to block his punch and throw yours at the same time. Your fist starts after his but lands first. Come on, boy! Fight! A boxing fight! You have to win it with your guts!

—That's good, Monsieur Gonzales. With the guts—I have understood!

—The bell! Look, he is rising up after you! It's a sign!

—Hey, boy? Hey, answer me! Come on! Wake up! Hey you, give him more sponge—now!

—Monsieur Gonzales, is he OK? Do you need anything? The doctor is coming.

—No, it's going to be all right. He just blinked. It's a sign!

17

Pride?

—Dad, what are all these grown-up men doing dressed with women's clothes, and why do they march like that?

—They are men, but they consider themselves and want to be seen as women!

—Ah! But then, why do they expose their bottoms? Women don't expose their bottoms like that for everybody to see. It is not decent!

—No, real women don't need to show their bottoms. At least, most of them!

—They are wearing curious clothes. They are not nice!

—They believe they are!

—But then, why parade like that? It is not Shrove Tuesday!

—They just want to show that they exist and that they deserve respect like everyone else because many people make fun of them. Indeed, it is provocative.

—"Provocative"?

—Yes. They do it on purpose to draw attention!

—Ah well. So you have to get naked to draw the attention of others?

—Not necessarily. There are more intelligent ways, but they are free to do it!

—Dad, why are there men and women?

—This is just how it is in nature. It is the same for all living creatures. There are two sexes—males and females—so that they can make children when they want. I have already explained this to you with the little seed that the father puts into the mother. Don't you remember?

—But these ones in the parade, how do they do the little-seed thing? Do they not want children?

—Actually, some of them want children, and it complicates things!

—But you cannot replace the mommies though.

—Yes, you need mommies—so far! People can also adopt children when they cannot make babies themselves, and in a few cases, some people buy them or even get them made by others.

—Buy them? There are people selling children?

—To some extent, yes.

—Dad, are you going to sell me? Did you buy me?

—No, my darling—certainly not! Your mom and me, we made you with love, and we did not need anybody else.

—And the daddies, can you replace them?

—Yes, it is possible. One can also buy little seeds and, with the help of doctors, place them where they need to be if a mommy does not want a dad or if the dad does not have enough little seeds.

—Then the daddies will not be necessary?

—I hope not because they are not just here to supply the little seeds.

—Dad, I don't want to have a dad who parades like that and exposes his bottom. Come on, Dad! We should leave!

*1. Shrove Tuesday—a traditional day for a masked parade

18

Modern Art

Dedicated to Joël Dufour

—Look at this painting. Is that not original?

—It is an infamous squiggle! It looks like a two-year-old child has enjoyed himself while playing with a pen. What is this horror called?

—*Jail*! But with a mind like yours, you will never understand anything about modern art!

—Ah! Because there is something to understand?

—Of course! Listen to what the exposition's booklet is saying: *"Jail* perfectly illustrates the stress of the artist in front of the blank canvas. The convolutions, at first harmonious, collide with the limits of the canvas and become more and more rough with the rising of the anguish. The artist is a prisoner like a fly in a closed bottle. It bumps into the glass sides without being able to find a way out!"

—Well, I say, this—you just had to find it!

—My poor friend, you are still thinking of the figurative! A painting is not a photograph. It does tell a story and expresses feelings!

—Ah, yes! And what does this little black line do? What does it mean?

—I don't know. It is not included in the commentary. Probably an omission.

—Wait, I am going to scratch a bit to see.

—No, don't touch it! You cannot do that! It is a work of art! *No!*

—Now see there. I scratched and it is gone. It was not paint.

—Then what was it?

—A paintbrush's hair that had been sticking! Let's go on with the visit.

—Look at this one. It is impressive, no?

—I don't see much difference with the other one! What's it called this time?

—*Self-portrait*!

—Dear! By luck, it is not figurative because with a face like that, the poor guy could not dare to get out of his place unnoticed! What does the booklet say?

—"*Self-portrait* is a powerful and realistic masterpiece that is some sort of picture from inside. The entangling of the lines evokes the convolutions of the brain and the paths of the ideas that interconnect before being expressed. It is the mechanism of the complexity and individuality of the mind that the artist has grasped in all its intimacy. A true graphic performance!"

—And some people believe in this bullshit and buy these crusts (*1).

—Yes, this painter is actually quite in fashion, highly rated, and rather expensive!

—In fashion, my foot! Well, keep going. There is one more painting by the same artist. It is promising!

—Come on, don't be so narrow-minded.

—He must have had some canvas and paint left over and used them to make a bit more money! Here! Look precisely. I recognize the scribble of your genius. This time, it looks like a school blackboard at the end of a geometry lesson. What is the title?

—*The Fulfilling of Senses.*

—Ah yes, indeed it is going to be full. Read me the comment first so that I can have a good laugh!

—OK, listen: "With *The Fulfilling of Senses*, the artist succeeded in facing the challenge of including both the space and the time on the flatness of the canvas. Starting from simple points—synonymous with immobility or, eventually, death—it goes in all directions and creates an effervescence of life when a point starts to move and becomes a line, and then this line, by the variations of its curves, can even go back in time and cross its own past. The space/time circles then rise in the picture to pop up at the surface like champagne bubbles in a cup. A sidereal artwork (*2)!"

—Now, here we are: sidereal, space, and time—nothing less! This guy believes he is Einstein, in addition. Was it not Einstein who said that human stupidity is more infinite than the universe? He certainly got that right!

—Now, look there—down in the right corner. There is again something curious. What can it be? It looks like some black points. No, no—don't try to scratch them! They mention these points in the comment, remember? They are crucial to the significance of this work!

—Too late! Well, no—it is not paint. It came away easily with my fingernail.

—Then what is it?

—Oh, just a bit of fly dirt!

*1. *Crusts*—the French use *croûtes* as a pejorative word for ugly paintings.
*2. *Sidereal*—"out of the world"

19

Robbed Thieves!

To revenge the poor relationships I experienced with my successive bankers.

—Good afternoon, Monsieur! How can I help you today?

—I would like to make a withdrawal!

—Very well. You have an account with us? And I will also need proof of your identity.

—It is not under my name!

—Then you have an authorized delegation of power. What is the name, please?

—Smith and Wesson!

—Wait a moment while I look through the files. Smith and Wesson? Are you sure? No, sorry—we don't have that.

—I am sorry too, but I have it right here. When I open my coat, see for yourself!

—Ah, indeed I can see it. Effectively, it is a power. Can I ask which model it is, if you will allow me?

—A .357 Magnum! But don't try to gain time by talking. I want a hundred thousand euros in small bills!

—Alas, Monsieur, this is impossible—even with your power!

—How can I believe that? There are millions in this bank, no?

—Probably, but not here at the public reception counters. We have only the cash for the day. For such a big withdrawal, one has to make a request at least twenty-four hours in advance. Did you make such a request?

—Of course not! Are you kidding me or what? Come on, show the dough!

—Please, listen to me, Monsieur. For such an amount, I will need to go to the safe, and even for the staff, we need authorization. Besides that, it will draw attention, suspicion, alarm, etc. And you will be immediately arrested. If I may be so bold as to give you advice, you should content yourself with what I have here now if you want to get out of here with some profit.

—And how much do you have in the box? I don't take coins. They are too heavy to run with!

—I cannot say exactly, but something around ten to fifteen thousand at the most. You will have to be happy with that!

—OK, well, let's do that. Put the bills in an envelope! And no dirty tricks!

—Don't be afraid, Monsieur! We have received special instructions to deal with this sort of situation, and we are committed to doing nothing that could put our customers at risk. That includes you, by the way!

—OK, get the bucks. I am watching you!

—Wait a minute. While I am preparing your money, can I ask you about your escape plan?

—Well, I will start running and lose myself in the crowd.

—Ooh la la, and what will happen if I sound the alarm? The safety cameras will follow you, and within five minutes, the cops will have you arrested. Not a very smart plan, indeed, and very dangerous!

—So what would you do?

—Here, listen. Just do a discharge—

—"A discharge"? You fool! I am not going to shoot you.

—No, not that kind of discharge, but a document signed by you that will certify that I have given you the money.

—And what good will that do?

—With a discharge document, I can prove that you left with twenty-thousand euros and the insurance will refund the bank!

—Twenty-thousand euros? You said there were only fifteen thousand at the most.

—Yes, I said that, but the extra five thousand are for me!

—YOU!

—Yes, me. When you think about it, I have acted as your financial advisor, no? And this is my fee for this case—fifteen thousand for you, five thousand for me!

—But that would be a daylight robbery!

—Coming from you, that is nearly a compliment! It is a deal-or-no-deal. Your choice! You sign the discharge, and I give you your envelope, set aside five thousand for myself, and wait until you are truly gone before ringing the alarm.

—This is the most crazy deal that I have ever made. How can I trust you?

—It is that or nothing. So?

—OK. Give me this discharge document. I will sign it. I will take the risk!

—Don't sign with your own name, you fool! Use "Smith and Wesson." That will do. Here! Very good. Here is your envelope with your money. You can go now. No bloodshed and everybody is happy. Thank you, Monsieur, for using our services. Feel free to come back when you want. No need to hurry. Goodbye and good luck!

—Yes, Monsieur Director, a holdup! He demanded a hundred thousand euros. I managed to negotiate for twenty thousand, and everything went well.

—Bravo, Monsieur. In the end, it seems that you have saved us eighty thousand euros.

—Yes, I suppose you could say that.

—Very good. You know, a holdup with firearms, shots, police, etc.— this would not have been good for the public image of our bank. You played your part really well. I shall see that the board of directors rewards you accordingly for your merit. I shall propose to them that they pay you a special bonus of five thousand. They cannot really refuse.

—Ah! Thank you so much, Monsieur Director! It is really a pleasure to work in this bank!

20

Metro, Boulot, (*1) Hobos

Dedicated to this guy around the corner who always gives me a bad conscience.

—Hey! What are you doing here? This is my spot!

—Excuse me. I did not know. I am a newcomer in this corner.

—Yes, but it is still my spot. I have been here every day for months. Where did you come from, for a start? I have never seen you around.

—I am a migrant.

—A migrant? That's what we needed! A migrant from where? From Africa?

—Yes, from the Sahel.

—Wow! It is not exactly next door! But you should have stayed home. Look at me. You can see that I am a hobo. Although I am from this country, I am jobless and forced to beg here at the metro exit.

—Well, I will go and find myself another place.

—Wait a minute. Sit down here on my bench—because this is MY bench, you know. Here, have a drink on me before going. I have a bottle of 3 Stars Red in my bag. We shall have a little chat. I have not many people to talk with.

—Thank you. Indeed, it's been a while since I have downed anything.

—That's no surprise with the way you are looking. Here, take this piece of sausage with the wine! So you are a migrant?

—Well, yes. My country has been a complete mess since you colonized and then decolonized us. For the poor, it does not make any difference!

—Bof! All of this—I have nothing to do with it. The colonies—those were for the rich people. You see the result: we are on the same pavement now!

—Yeah, but you—you have a begging spot! Are you doing well here?

—Bof! There are some good and bad days. Sometimes I make a dozen euros—enough for some grub!

—A dozen euros! But with us, one is RICH with less than that!

—Rich? Dear, you don't need much! It is true that I have a good spot: a metro exit, a warm air-ventilation outlet not far away, and a resto du Coeur (*2) around the corner, and sometimes I get scooped up by the patrol when it gets too cold, and they make me spend the night in a shelter. But from there, to say that I am rich, there is a long way!

—You even have a resto! What is that? A resto du Coeur?

—A guy named Coluche started this thing with a few friends for blokes like us. It is like a soup kitchen but better. We get real plates and glasses, and you can get your fill for free.

—Was he a politician?

—Of course not! The politicians? Don't expect anything from them! They are too dumb for that! He was a humorist. He was a pain in the ass for the mighty and made the good guys laugh. A good dude if ever there was one! There are not many of them left!

—But how did you land here on this pavement, if I can ask?

—Bof! It is quite a classic story. I had a good job. The company went bankrupt. I lost my job, then unemployment and unpaid bills. We got evicted from our apartment. My wife went away with another guy. The children are being cared for by social welfare. I took to drinking to forget. And you?

—Also a classic story. The riots, the war, and the plunder. The village was attacked. The women were raped or enslaved. I found myself all alone and was forced to enlist. I escaped and hid in a boat. Luckily, they did not find me. I disembarked—without papers, of course—and now I am here, trying to survive. I don't want to get involved in drug trafficking, and I live on the street. That's it!

—Dear, you had your share too! Indeed, we are very much alike. Finally, huh?

—We are both in the shit! Bloody damned world of shit, it is!

—You sure got that right, mate!

—Well, I have to go now. I must find myself something today. Thank you for the snack. Bye-bye! Maybe we shall see each other again!

—Wait, wait a minute. I just got an idea. You see, at this metro station, people get down using one side of the stairway and go out using the other side, and me, I am alone and can cover only one side. If you were on the other side, we could both control the people going in and out. What do you think about that, man?

—I think it is a bloody good idea! But are you sure it will not be a problem for you? I certainly don't want to force your hand!

—Don't knock yourself out, my boy! If I say so, it is because it is fine! And then, from time to time, we could have a chat and a drink on my bench. Right? Come on, settle yourself!

—Well then, I can't believe it! Thank you for giving me a chance and sharing your spot!

—Bof! You know, one shares more easily when one owns nothing!

1. *Boulot*—"job"

21

Monsieur My Representative!

I am quite happy that you could get a seat at the Parliament. Having to stand during all those endless sessions—that would be really asking too much. I hope that you will have good neighbors so that you will not get bored and can share a few good jokes with them. If necessary, if you have missed some of the debates because of a little reparative nap, after the blowout of the day, they will tell you what you have to vote for. If need be, they could do it for you if you are busy somewhere else.

Concerning the commission's work, don't worry. Anyways, as it is useless, it will be better for you to leave this to the others and use your time to answer your post and read your mail. You can also ask your attaché to do that. He is not there to twiddle his thumbs.

On the other hand, it would be good if one could see you more often on the screen of the TV chain of the Parliament, pretending to take notes or, even better, addressing the Speaker with colorful names or slamming your desk. You have to make yourself noticed. Wearing a yellow jacket does not mean that you have the stuff to be a minister.

I noticed that in recent times, you had a tendency to become plump. Of course, it is difficult to deal with all these commitments and all these receptions. A politician must not have only a big mouth but also a good liver and a good stomach. Not having to pay for your bills, you have to know how to pay yourself without compromising your health!

I also noticed that it has been quite a long time since you turned your vest and changed sides (*1). I hope that it is not due to the consequences of the above point or that this cloth has become too tight or prematurely worn-out by too many turnovers. On this chapter, I have been told that some representatives receive free suits, shoes, etc., from luxury brands. Maybe you should make an application.

Furthermore, I am writing this letter now because I only recently got interested in politics—after having participated at the gilets jaunes (*2) demonstrations. I became aware that my fundamental qualities were not being used at their fair value. Indeed, I know how to walk around a roundabout and follow the others who are shouting slogans. My training as a jobless person prepared me for sitting for hours and doing nothing. I am a solid eater and a good drinker. I know how to talk and say nothing and work to do nothing. I know how to close my eyes and open my ears. I am very good at spending other people's money.

This is why I would like to follow your example and benefit from your advice and support to engage in politics. I would really like to be a member of your team, and I am quite confident that, in view of the references and qualities exposed here, you will not miss to think of me if some opportunity arises.

With the insurance of my deepest devotion.

Your Servitor

*1. In France, when a politician changes sides, it is said that they "turn their vest."
*2. Gilets jaunes (yellow jerseys) did a number of demonstrations against the government in France in 2018 and 2019.

22

Dear Elector, Dear Friend!

Your letter has raised all my attention. It is indeed quite rare to find people who are conscious of the true difficulties of the task of being a representative of the nation. Indeed, you have to fight to win a seat, but you also have to spend your time on defending it. Yes, these Parliament sessions that finish late into the night are exhausting, not to mention the many commitments of the charge.

As you have very well understood, one has to sacrifice one's private life and sometimes one's own opinions—not to mention the pernicious atmosphere that makes today's friends become tomorrow's enemies.

After what you told me, I realized that you indeed possess some excellent features and a background that would justify one getting interested in you. Your indisputable qualities deserve to express themselves somewhere other than a roundabout or a boulevard. You are young, and I always personally campaign to help the youth, especially the enterprising youth.

In this perspective, I am going to ask you to liaise with my attaché, who will look toward finding for you a place in my squad. Perhaps, at the beginning, you will have to start with putting up posters or exchanging a few punches with the opposition's teams. But one has to start from the base and show what he is capable of before climbing the ranks.

But, as in politics, things are sometimes moving fast (at least in what concerns the promotions). I don't doubt that with a profile and references like yours, you will rapidly become an actor of the public life.

Concerning my seat, however, I have in mind to keep it for some time, but you will have all my support and the support of our party to conquer yours when the opportunity will come.

We do need people like you—competent and selfless!

In this perspective, I send you, my dear future colleague, the insurance of my highest consideration.

Your Deputy

Postscript: Concerning the suits, you are right. I shall meet with some names that have been given to me. They probably have some surpluses or will give me the good addresses.

23

The Unfair Strength of the Law
Quote from President François Mitterrand
Dedicated to Jean Giraud, who introduced me
to the "philosophic" way of fishing

—Hep, Monsieur! What are you doing here? Fishing is forbidden here during this season!

—Ah! I did not know. Are you sure?

—All the more for I am the game warden of this village. I am sorry, but I have to charge you a fine!

—But . . . well, indeed, I am not really fishing!

—How is that? Is that not a fishing rod? And a line with a floater? Don't try to play games with me! I have been observing you for quite a while, and you are fishing.

—If you have been observing me, you must have seen that I did not catch anything.

—The matter is not to catch or not to catch. It is the ACT of fishing that is forbidden. Do you have an ID with you?

—Wait . . . yes. Here it is.

—So it is you, Monsieur Pierre Jambart?

—Yes, it's me, but to tell the truth, I have to explain something. I am not fishing in the real sense of the term. I am just dipping my line and my floater in the water, but at the end of the line, there is no bait and not even a hook. You can see that when I reel back my line.

—By George, you are right! But what on earth is this story about? Something is wrong somewhere! Are you fishing, or are you not fishing?

—I am not fishing! On the contrary, I am protecting the fish!

—WHAT!

—Yes! I come here. I throw them some food, pieces of bread or some kibble, and after that, I mount my gear and wet my line. The fish know me and wait for me as I come nearly every day.

—There is something that I don't get. Are you sure you are OK in your mind?

—I am fine. Indeed, I am pretending to be fishing to prevent other fishermen from coming to this spot and catching my fish!

—Goodness gracious, this is quite peculiar! You are special, one can say! And you keep standing there for hours to wet your line and do nothing else?

—Yes. It is wonderful. It helps me relax. I am a novelist. I need to let my thoughts wander to imagine the stories I am going to write. And I am also observing nature. It is better than yoga. Besides that, it helps me build relationships.

—Build relationships?

—Well, yes. The walkers stop to look at me fish. Some ask if they are biting, and usually, they stay a moment to discuss fishing or nature. Others observe my floater and wait for a bite. After a while, they get discouraged, and they go away and wish me good luck. There are some who take pictures. For them, I belong to the landscape.

—OK, that's good, but nevertheless, you are in breach, and I have to draw up a charge sheet. If people saw us, what would they think if I didn't do my duty? My authority is at stake!

—Bah! Do as you wish. You are the one in charge of enforcing the law.

—Yes, but it is not always simple. This situation is proof of that. Well, I will summarize what I have written so that you can sign the sheet: "I, Cyprien Letourneur, acting as game warden of the municipality, have this day caught the so-called Pierre Oscar Jambart in action of fishing at the place known as La Sauleraie—in breach of the municipal edict regulating this activity. The above-mentioned having admitted the facts, he has been issued with a comprehensive report with a fine of 0 (zero) euro, which he has paid immediately." Here, Monsieur. Please sign down there.

—But wait—zero euro? What, is that for a joke?

—Well, Monsieur, it is quite simple. You are fishing without wanting to catch any fish, and I am issuing you a fine without wanting to take any money. Is that not what is fitting for this situation?

24

The Horse Whisperer

—Hi, can I see Old Pa Lemadec?

—I shall look for him, but he may be taking his daily nap. He is getting old, you know!

—He must be VERY old. I have always known him as being old. How old can he be now?

—Something close to ninety, but he is still very active and very clear-minded.

—OK. See if he can receive me but leave him alone if he is sleeping. I can wait. Thank you.

—You are lucky. He just woke up. He is happy to see you. Come in, please.

—Hello, Old Pa. How are you doing?

—Monsieur Taffart, what a surprise! I have not seen you for so long. I was thinking you had forgotten me.

—Certainly not, but you know how it is with our business. It's a 24-7 job.

—Yes, it is! How is your racing stable doing?

—Not too well, and this is the reason for my visit.

—Ah! Tell me.

—Indeed, we are deep in the shit. We have had an incredible succession of unlucky events and poor results for nearly two seasons now. Our best champion broke one leg during training and had to be sent back for reproduction. Then we had this bloody illness, some sort of equine flu, that lasted weeks despite the antibiotic treatment. That went on for months, and nearly all the horses were contaminated. They are still recovering very slowly, and of course, they cannot be trained properly, and they cannot race. The few survivors are unfortunately not our best ones and can barely stand on their legs. So we have not been winning anything since the start of this season.

—I reckon these bloody animals are really fragile and can bring a lot of trouble! Is that all?

—No! As the cherry on the cake, we are drowning in debt. If we don't win any prize money before the end of the month, we will be bankrupt. I will have to sell the horses and the stables to pay the debts and the indemnities for the employees and start to find myself a new job!

—Are you here to ask me for some money? I would happily help, but as a pensioner, you know that I don't have much.

—No, not at all. I am just here for advice. You are famous for knowing all the tricks in the book concerning horse racing. Maybe you can do something. In two weeks, we have a grand prix in Paris. I have entered two horses, but I am afraid that they don't have even the smallest chance of winning or placing. That will probably be my last race as a horse trainer.

—Dear, and I am your last resort. But I am no sorcerer. That's what you need—a wizard!

—Some people told me that it was what you were called in your time!

—People are always exaggerating. I only had a few successes, I reckon!

—Please, can you help me?

—Well, you are a good man, but I am also thinking about your horses and all your staff. Maybe I can try something, but don't get too excited. I am not sure if it will work. Which one is actually the better of your two horses?

—Daisy Belle, a three-year mare. But she is quite tricky to manage and has never won anything—and probably never will!

—Don't say that! What is wrong with her?

—She is very whimsical. She can run fast. I have seen her do so during training, but it seems that she does not WANT to win.

—WHAT! She does not WANT to win? That's peculiar!

—Yes. She enjoys running after the other horses, but she never takes the lead. She stays behind the pack, and when she crosses the line, she is as fresh as a just-caught fish. And whenever the jockey tries to boost her with the horsewhip, she always gets upset and slows down on purpose!

—Can you tell me more about her? What does she like the most and what does she hate the most, for example?

—She is crazy about apples—probably because she comes from Normandy. She will smell an apple in your hand from the other side of the paddock and come running. But she hates dogs, and when there is one around, she just runs away at full speed!

—This is quite interesting. Could you bring her here and let her stay with me for a few days? I need to talk to her.

—WHAT? TALK TO HER?

—Yes, talk to her. What is wrong with that?

—But this is not a Hollywood movie! You cannot TALK to horses!

—That, we shall see, but if you want me to help you, you have to give me free rein and not ask questions. OK?

—OK. Do as you wish. I shall bring you the horse this afternoon! I am going now. Thank you for agreeing to help—whatever the result may be. You don't want to talk to Chenapan, the other horse?

—No, it will not be necessary, but you crossing your fingers might be a good idea. Just do that!

—Now, here we are. The grand prix starts in less than one hour. Thank you for coming, Old Pa Lemadec. Is everything OK?

—Yes, Monsieur Taffart. I just need to have a last chat with the two jockeys of your horses to confirm our strategy. Ah, here they are! Please, come with me for one minute, boys.

—Can I come too?

—No, sorry. It is better that you know nothing about it. No offense, of course!

—OK. You have free rein, I know!

—OK, boys, listen again to our plan. Right at the start, you will get out Chenapan as a cannonball. He MUST take the lead! Have you got those crushed apples in your pockets and under the saddle? Yes? Great!

—Yes, we smell like we just bathed in a cask of apple cider!

—So you will lead the race at least until halfway—more, if you can—and because of the attractive apple smell, Daisy Belle will follow her stable partner, not the other horses. The pace must be very fast, and the other jockeys will cautiously follow at some distance, not knowing what is going on.

—Yes, but at that pace, Chenapan will not last longer than a kilometer at best, and then he will slow down suddenly.

—That is expected, but it is when you, with Daisy belle, will come to play your role.

—But she will not want to take the lead. She has never done it!

—I bet she will if you do what I say. When you see Chenapan starting to collapse, just start barking at your horse like a mad dog—as loud and as aggressive as you can.

—The other jockeys will think I have gone insane! Is that allowed?

—Who cares? You can encourage your horse with your voice, whatever the sounds you are producing, no?

—But I have never heard of something like this before!

—Do it. That's all. Remember that I am in charge. I trained her to react to that last week.

—OK, OK. I shall do it, don't worry. Besides, it might even be fun!

—It will, believe me. OK, let's go, you two.

—Here, Monsieur Taffart, don't be so nervous. Everything will be fine.

—Daisy Belle looks nervous too. I have never seen her like that before.

—It is because she knows!

—She knows what?

—She knows about the situation—the possible bankruptcy and everything else, especially the fact that this race could be your last one! She knows that she HAS to win.

—You are kidding me! How could she know such things?

—Because I told her!

—Here they come now. They are under the starter's orders. Look, Old Pa Lemadec! Now the gate is lifted. Here they go! Wow!

—What happened? At my age, I cannot see well, even with binoculars. Tell me.

—Chenapan has gone out of the gate like an arrow and has taken the lead and . . .

—And?

—Daisy Belle is following just behind his tail. She looks like she's taking it easy, but what a pace! They cannot keep going like that! It is suicidal!

—How far are they now?

—They are reaching the halfway mark of the race. Still in the same order.

—Good!

—No, not good because Chenapan looks tired now. Yes, he is clearly slowing down. The others are coming. There are still four hundred meters to go! OH!

—What?

—Daisy Belle! She is coming! She is overtaking Chenapan! She is LEADING!

—Good! How long to go now?

—Here they come. You can see by yourself now. They are just going out of the last bend. Daisy Belle is leading by one length. Three hundred meters to go! Come on, Daisy Belle! Come on! Dear, I cannot believe it! She is now in front by two lengths!

—Two hundred meters! She is still holding the two lengths! But the others are producing their efforts and are under their whips.

—Go, Daisy Belle, go! The jockey is pushing her but is not using his whip. One hundred meters to go! They are closing in on her, but she still has more than one length.

—Daisy Belle! DAISY BELLE! YEAH! SHE WON IT! YEAH! Old Pa Lemadec, you are a genius!

—Come on, Old Pa. It's time to go to bed. You had a hard day at the races. You are not used to this anymore.

—Yes, Old Ma, but it was fun!

—What did you do at the end? I have been told about the trick with the crushed apples and the barking, but this would not have been enough to make Daisy Belle keep going at that pace. What did you do? Be honest. Tell me. I shall not say anything to anybody.

—Well, look at this little brown bottle. I got it from my own grandfather, who was already in the horse business. You put a few drops of this in a horse's food for a week, and soon you have another animal.

—But it is doping! It is forbidden!

—Guess what, I don't exactly know what are in there, but all the products are not on the doping list. I have tested it. Don't worry. All that I know is that it probably has gunpowder, hot chili, wasp venom, and a few similar things.

—And you give that to a horse?

—Yes, and if it does not explode, it usually crosses the line a winner! I have successfully used it myself several times in my trainer career. I wonder if it could work on humans?

—Old Pa Lemadec, you are just an old fool! But what about this story of "talking" to the horse?

—Believe it or not, I DID TALK to Daisy Belle!

—Come on! But why?

—Because she is not only a horse but also a female. You cannot expect to obtain anything from the members of this gender if you are not able to talk to them properly. So I talked to Daisy Belle!

—And she listened and understood?

—Who knows? But the result is here. You cannot deny this!

—Old Pa Lemadec, you are just an old fart! I remember how you were talking to me when you asked me to marry you.

—So you see, it worked already! But I swear I did not use the little brown bottle! Ha ha!

25

Don't Rock the Boat!

Dedicated to a cop who happens to be a good friend of mine—Robert!

—Lecoin? Ah yes, I wanted to have a word with you.

—On what subject, Monsieur Superintendent?

—How long have you been out of the police school and assigned to our squad?

—Only six months, Monsieur Superintendent!

—Yes, that's about the time. Well, we have to talk about how you are doing. There are some issues!

—Issues, Monsieur Superintendent? But I am doing my best, I can assure you!

—I don't doubt it, and there lies the heart of the issue. You are overdoing it!

—How is that possible, Monsieur Superintendent? We have a lot to do, and we are undermanned!

—I know, I know. But this is not a reason to be overzealous. As a matter of fact, it does disturb some people, and I have received some complaints.

—Complaints? From whom?

—Well, let's start with this one. It is the college principal's. It seems that you entered his school's boundary to perform a police action without having made a request and getting authorization. You know the law on the matter. This complaint is supported by a petition signed by some teachers.

—Gosh, that's a good one! I was patrolling the street when I heard a scream that came from the schoolyard. There was an older guy menacing a young one with a knife and demanding him to hand over his mobile phone. I went in, and the guy with the knife ran away. That's all!

—Alas, no, that's not all! The principal says that this was an intrusion and interference in the establishment's policy and that you should have made a request via the school office and your hierarchy.

—The hierarchic way! That's ridiculous! That would have taken at least a week! So the principal would rather have a student get injured or even worse, and the petition's teachers too? It is no surprise that these same people cry or start a strike when they are themselves menaced by a student holding a gun! It is much in fashion nowadays!

—Monsieur Lecoin, it is not for us to judge these matters. The fact is that you have put us in a sensitive situation concerning this institution!

—And the parents of the assaulted student? They said nothing?

—I am afraid that they have not been asked to express their mind.

—Probably because people were too busy trying to find excuses for the aggressor!

—Come on, Inspector Decoin, you are making accusations without proof! Let us continue with the other concerns I have. Here is an anonymous complaint from someone residing in the Lenquette suburb.

—But this suburb does not belong to our sector!

—No! But you have intensified the patrols in the neighboring suburb of Bellevue, which is in our sector, and made the business of the local drug dealers difficult. These dealers have now retreated to Lenquette, making the lives of the inhabitants there impossible because the gang of Bellevue is considering this as an invasion of their territory, and the two gangs are now continuously fighting. This person says that before long, there will be casualties.

—And that will be my fault! That takes the cake!

—I did not say that. But you have to be aware that peace is all about maintaining a fragile balance between diverse communities. So you have to take care and think about all the consequences before starting anything.

—If I understand you right, Monsieur Superintendent, you are suggesting that one should better do nothing in these situations!

—I did not say that either, but you will realize when you will have enough experience that one cannot always behave like a cowboy, especially in our suburban areas. But I kept the best for the end because it is a complaint coming from our supervising authorities, the prefecture and the Ministry of Internal Affairs.

—The prefecture? The ministry? How is that possible? What have I done?

—In fact, it is not officially a complaint because there is nothing written, as you can imagine, but I have received some strong recommendations from some very senior officials.

—Monsieur Superintendent, enlighten me. What are they blaming me for?

—Well, you have to realize that your continual activity these last six months has resulted in many statements, reports, police detentions, etc. Your efforts, therefore, had the consequence of making the crime statistics explode—not only in our sector but also in the whole area. We are now considered as an area with a high rate of insecurity. The journalists have run with it and knocked out stupid articles that analyze the possible reasons. There was even a TV crew who covered the story. Of course, they dramatized things—so much so that there is a risk that the politicians will get involved and turn it into a national scandal where the opposition will find it easy to say "What are the police doing?" and demand the head of the concerned minister. I have received phone calls asking me what was going on with us and insisting that I stop this circus immediately! So you see the picture now!

—I am dumbstruck, Mister Superintendent! All this fuss because I just wanted to do my job! It's incredible!

—Alas, yes, my young friend. One does not teach you these things at the police school! I am sorry to rid you of your illusions because I, like you, was a young inspector myself. This is why I wanted to have a chat with you. If you keep going like this, we will both be transferred for service reasons— you and me. You have more to lose than me because I am at the end of my career. For the moment, I shall try to cushion the blow by pretending that there have been some statistic errors, but you—I shall give you a new responsibility inside the department. Don't take it wrongly. It is to protect you. Later, you will understand, and you will be thankful.

—Monsieur Superintendent, I certainly appreciate your interest in me and thank you for your advice. You can be sure that I will not forget it.

—That's right, that right! You will also see that, with experience, one can be a good cop like one can be a good sailor, especially when you have to go against the wind.

—Without rocking the boat! I have understood, Monsieur Superintendent!

26

Luggage or Not Luggage?

Dedicated to British Airways.

—Good afternoon, Monsieur! Where are you going?

—Good afternoon, Madame. Sydney and then Auckland.

—Well, please give me your ticket. You will have a stop in Singapore.

—There it is!

—And your passport?

—Here!

—Very good! Can you put your luggage on the scale?

—That's done!

—Fifty-seven kilograms. OK, but there is a problem.

—How is that? We are allowed to have sixty kilograms. That was in your advertisement, and it is the reason that made me choose your company.

—Sixty kilograms, this is correct, but it must be only one piece of luggage!

—WHAT? What sort of ridiculous story is this?

—Yes, the regulation stipulates *ONE* authorized piece of luggage with a maximum weight of sixty kilograms.

—But it is silly. When have you ever wandered around with sixty-kilogram pieces of luggage? Do you see people dealing with that in the trains, the taxis, or the stairs?

—I cannot do anything about it, Monsieur. The rule says *ONE* luggage. Here, you can read it. And you have two suitcases. I cannot help it!

—But when I came one month ago, I had the same luggage, and there was no problem.

—I certainly believe you, Monsieur, but people at check-in sometimes allow different things. You were lucky. At this counter, it is *ONE* piece of luggage!

—Yes, I was lucky to have dealt with some intelligent people and not with an idiotic regulation.

—Monsieur, I cannot allow you to say that.

—Well! And now, what are we doing?

—You can still try to transfer the contents of one suitcase into the other.

—How will that work? Unpack all my personal belongings in the airport—in front of everybody? Thank you for showing the respect due to your customers. And even if, by some miracle, I would successfully fit everything in one, the seams are not made for that and will burst open. And what am I going to do with the empty suitcase? Throw it away? Thank you, but no—it was expensive enough!

—I can do nothing for you, Monsieur. Please, can you step aside? The other customers are waiting.

—Yes and they can also see how you are treating me. You are a bit embarrassed, perhaps! No, I am going to stay here!

—Monsieur, if you persist, I am going to call the security!

—Thank you for treating me like a terrorist! Indeed, *ME*—I have an idea. Look. I have here two straps, and I am going to use them to bind solidly the two suitcases together. Then it will become only one piece of luggage.

—Monsieur, I cannot accept this. You are circumventing the regulation!

—WHAT? This is now clearly *ONE* piece of luggage. I don't see anything in your regulation that stipulates the shape and the parts of a luggage. Do you need now to travel with a lawyer and quibble about the proper meanings of the words?

—Monsieur, I shall have to call for our station manager to settle the matter.

—Just do that, please! Call him! Let's hope that he will be a little more comprehensive.

—Monsieur, this is our station manager. He wants to have a word with you privately.

—No, not privately. Me, I have nothing to hide, and I want the other customers of this shit company to serve as witnesses.

—Please, Monsieur, calm down! What is the problem?

—The madame here at the counter refuses to admit this as *ONE* piece of luggage because your bloody regulation allegedly requires me to have only one. She wants me to transfer all my belongings into one suitcase, which will likely burst open during the trip, and abandon the other. Bravo for the service and the way you respect your customers!

—I see, Monsieur, I see!

—Precisely, and if you see so well, I ask you to take a look at the nearby counter where that woman just dropped a baby buggy inside which she fixed a bag with packaging tape. That luggage has been accepted without question by the check-in hostess in spite of the fact that it is clearly made of two parts.

—I see! Yes, but it's for a baby!

—I am sorry that I am not a baby myself. But one can rarely see babies moving around with sixty-kilogram pieces of luggage. Nevertheless, I suppose that the regulation is the same for everybody, no?

—I see, Monsieur, I see! You are going to Auckland?

—I am trying to, and I am traveling with some quite-famous local sports stars. It is very likely that the press and TV will meet us upon our arrival. It will certainly be a good opportunity to do to this company the publicity it deserves!

—Monsieur, this is blackmail!

—It is no more blackmail than your advertising is misleading and your ways are unpleasant!

—Well, Monsieur, if you would agree to wait a moment, please. I will see what I can do.

—Monsieur?

—Yes, Monsieur Manager?

—Monsieur, it is now OK and sorted out. You can check in your luggage the way you want and even separate the two suitcases, which is, by the way, also more practical for the staff! Allow me to express regret for this incident, and I hope you accept our apologies. I wish you and your champions a pleasant flight.

—Monsieur, thank you for sorting out this quarrel. I see that the other passengers waiting are also showing their satisfaction. Let's hope that they too will be treated properly. Goodbye, Monsieur.

Note of the author: This scene really happened one day at the Genève international airport. It just goes to show that the absurd is present in everyday reality. It seems that this company has made some progress, but I cannot personally attest to that, having systematically preferred other transporters since the incident.

27

On Patrol

—Sergeant, Sergeant! I have seen some guys up there in the village. They were wearing black djellabas (*1) and trying to run into the ruins.

—They must be hiding now and waiting for us to come.

—Hey! We are not going to move, are we? There is just open space between here and the ruins. They will shoot us down like rabbits!

—No, no! I am going to ask for a reconnaissance drone. Meanwhile, get to secure positions. Dig your individual holes immediately. Transmit the order to the others of the patrol. Quick!

—Here comes the drone, but what the hell is it doing?

—Shit! They shot it down! They know the trick now. So, Serg, what are we going to do now?

—Stay in your holes! I am going to ask for artillery support from our regimental battery.

—Fuck! That hit them hard! The shells have even gone down the minaret. What now?

—Get out of your holes and use the skirmishing positions.

—Hey! Watch out! We are under fire! It cannot be possible that there are still survivors in there!

—Quick! Back to the holes! I am going to ask for air support. Wait for orders!

—Sergeant! What are we doing here, and why are we at war with these nuts? They are at home here. They can do whatever they want.

—Not your problem, Corporal! Please avoid that sort of question!

—But, Serg, we are risking our hides! What for?

—That's enough of that! We are soldiers, and these are our orders. That's the point, OK?

—Here come the planes. They did not take long. A pair of fighter-bombers. Watch out! This is going to get hot. Spread a blue canvas so they see where we are!

—That's done, Serg! Holy shit! The planes are coming right at us!

—Don't worry, they use laser bombs. Those things are quite accurate!

—My god! Right on target! I would not like to be with those guys!

—Wait for the dust to settle so we can see something and then move forward to pick up their pieces.

—Shit! That can't be true! They are still shooting at us, and this time, they have a heavy machine gun. But how is that possible? They should have been reduced to a pulp!

—They must have underground bunkers.

—Then, Serg, it does not look good for us. It doesn't look like we shall remove them easily!

—I agree and certainly not without heavy losses. I am going to inform the command.

—Where is the command?

—Well, at the rear—in their air-conditioned bunkers and watching their computer screens.

—Couldn't they come here from time to time? They would probably see more than what's on their bloody screens!

—Shut up and do what I do. Wait for orders!

—Aye, aye, Chief!

—That's it! They have answered!

—Good! So we are retreating?

—Out of the question! They say they are going to send us some tanks.

—Fuck them, but the armored vehicles will not get into this village. The streets are too narrow and full of obstacles. Anyways, these guys have probably set mines everywhere. It is completely stupid!

—Serg! Look there! The tanks are coming! There are three of them! Damn it! One of them has just taken a point-blank hit. It is on fire. The bastards had a rocket launcher. The two other tanks are turning back. They are afraid of getting the same fate. Now then, Serg, we are alone again. We do what?

—We drop out, and we withdraw to the prepared-in-advance positions, as it is said in the books. After all, they can go to hell with their bloody war!

—Really, Sergeant! Is it you who just said that? The planes, the tanks, the bombs, the dead! It is true that this costs a lot, and in the end, for what result?

—Yes, but shut your bloody mouth, Corporal! This may be expensive, but we are here to make the price of a liter of petrol stay low. And just keep that between us, OK?

*1. *Djellaba*—a traditional woolen robe that is used in the Middle East and certain African countries.

28

Hierar . . . Shit!

—You wanted to see me, Monsieur Personnel Director?

—Yes, Monsieur Chassecourt. There is an internal problem concerning our department, and it concerns you.

—Ah! I am listening.

—Here it is. It has been reported to me that you have several times used the toilets that are restricted to the directors when there are toilets especially assigned for the personnel.

—This is possible, Monsieur Personnel Director, but it was certainly due to a situation of urgency—one where the personnel toilets were occupied.

—But it seems that you are a bit too often in urgency precisely. And to believe my information, you are in fact completely ignoring the rule and seem to prefer using the directorial toilets even when the ones allocated for you are free.

—I did not know that our toilets were under watch!

—No, this is not about being under watch, but the people who are working in the nearby office clearly see the comings and goings, and they simply answered my questions.

—A toilet is a toilet. In urgency, one can be confused, no?

—Actually, no! The directorial toilets, as you have certainly noticed by now, are more spacious, equipped with infrared heaters, and supplied with perfumed soft paper, according to the instructions relating to the comfort of the officials of category A—a category that is not yours, as far as I know.

—That's true. I admit it, Monsieur Director.

—In addition, Monsieur Lagrange, the sous-chef of the department and the one in charge of the administrative supplies, has signaled to me an abnormal and considerable increase of the consumption of toilet-paper model AD26 modified 43, which is the one we use for the directorial toilets, when the personnel toilets are only furnished with model AD18b. We have nearly consumed our annual allowance of the former!

—Ah well!

—Yes! And if we have to make a demand for a supplementary allowance, we shall be exposed to an internal inquiry that will look for the causes of this excessive consumption. This is highly disagreeable, as you can imagine.

—An inquiry? Effectively, I did not think about this eventuality!

—Indeed, you should have been thinking a little bit before giving free rein to your inclinations. Try to imagine the reaction of our department chief if he discovered that not only somebody is using his toilets but there is also an inquiry from the ministry coming to interrogate our staff on how many times we use the facilities, the time spent, the quantity of paper used, and God knows what else they need for their bloody reports.

—Monsieur Director, I could not imagine—

—Monsieur Chassecourt! You have belonged to this service for only a short time. You are young, but you should already know that in a good administration, everything is hierarchical and managed in consequence. Without that, it leaves the door open to chaos and havoc.

—Monsieur Director, please believe me when I say that I do regret and—

—I certainly do hope that you regret and that your comportment was not premeditated and disrespectful to your superiors. Considering your young age and inexperience, I shall wipe the slate clean this time and give you only an oral warning, which will stay between us, but I am now expecting your exemplary conduct on this matter, and I shall personally see that it is so.

—Monsieur Director, I thank you for your indulgence. From now on, I shall make sure to restrict my activities in this matter and control my administrative consumption.

—Very well, Monsieur Chassecourt. I am not holding you further. You can go back to your duties.

29

Ministerial Visit

—Monsieur Mayor, I have finished writing your speech for the visit of the minister of the circular evolutions and countermarch. Do you want to review it if you wish to make some corrections and get familiar with it?

—Thank you, Monsieur City Clerk. You were fast. I would like to do just that now as we still have a little time before he comes with all his entourage. Give me the paper, please! Thank you!

—Here, Monsieur Mayor! I wrote big letters so you don't have to use your glasses.

—You are working out all the details, indeed! Great! Let's see now:

"Monsieur Minister, Monsieur Deputy—"

—Ah! This one! He will be there? That idiot?

—Alas, yes, Monsieur Mayor! He has confirmed that he is going to attend all the planned events: the reception at the town hall, the inauguration of the new stand at the stadium, the visit at the college, the ceremony at the war memorial, and the wine reception with the veterans and the leading citizens.

—What a sticker, this deputy! And we belong to the same party! But he is scared to death that I could steal his seat, and he is always in the way to show his mug to the media!

Well, there is nothing we can do about that! Let's read further:

"Monsieur Subprefect, ladies and gentlemen, local representatives, and dear fellow citizens, on this memorable day, I am happy to welcome to our little community of Sainte Scolastique en Augiens one of the most obedient servants of our republic and a prominent member of the government, Monsieur Auguste Godillot, who also happens to be one of my best friends—"

—Hey! Are you not overdoing it a bit? This guy is an absolute bastard. He refused to take me into his ministerial cabinet and instead nominated his mistress's husband! Probably to thank him for playing the third wheel!

—I know, Monsieur Mayor, but we have to comply with the due decorum. It's not the time to settle accounts. The public will not understand.

—OK, but anyways, my time will come. Don't be afraid! He will not be a minister for long! Well, let's continue:

"Monsieur Auguste Godillot has come here in person, regardless of his extremely busy schedule, to inaugurate the new facilities of our sporting grounds and the new equipment of our college without forgetting to pay tribute to our glorious veterans—"

—Ah, you are talking! In fact, the old crab is here to prepare for the next elections and negotiate for alliances and local support. Therefore, they forced my hand so that he could come and make this inauguration.

—It's true, Monsieur Mayor! They left us no choice.

—This is again a publicity gimmick! Even the media organizations knew before us that he was coming. Any other governmental penguin could have done the job! Well, this is politics, and you know as much as I do about it!

—Yes, Monsieur Mayor, I know. The local representatives are here to do the job while the ones in high places, they fiddle and make the decisions.

—Well, we are not going to change the world now! Let's read the rest of your masterpiece!

"This program shows the concern of our community to build always closer ties between our enthusiastic youth and our elders, who deserve to be respected for their sacrifices during the wars. We want now to be prepared to win the battles of the future and keep maintaining for our population the way of life and the culture that are ours. But we want to do this without rejecting the external contributions. So long as they are in accordance with our values—"

—Ooh la la, Monsieur City Clerk, we'll be on a dangerous field there! All the do-gooders of the official thinking will scrutinize every word and try to catch me red-handed for tongue-slipping!

—Yes, but you also have to please everybody, and if you dodge the subject, they will complain that you did not take responsibility. Anyways, you know quite well what these speeches are worth! Nobody really cares!

—Yes, evidently. OK, let's finish now:

"Then, in my quality of mayor of this township, I wish you all a good welcome, and I invite you now to proceed toward our municipal sports ground for the second stage of this day. Long live to the Scolastique en Augiens, long live to the republic, long live to France!"

—So, Monsieur Mayor, do you want to change anything?

—No, that will do. Thank you! You have done a good job. A propos (*1), did you check if there was any risk of an incident happening? That would be embarrassing. No CGT demonstrations (*2)? No gilets jaunes?

—No, they are all busy somewhere else!

—And the Front National (*3)?

—They have a headache!

—And the teachers?

—They are all gone for holidays, as usual.

—The greens, the LGBT, the nurses, the truck drivers, and the peasants (*4)?

—No, they are not up to something at the moment!

—Well, but there will be nobody left! If there is no public, that will not look too good for us!

—No, we shall make do. The soccer teams, the children from the boarding school, the municipality employees, the war veterans—all of them will be there!

—These veterans, we don't have many left, and there are less of them every year. We shall have to find something to replace them soon.

—Don't worry! Indeed, there is no shortage of wars!

———

*1. *A propos*—"by the way"
*2. CGT (Confederation Générale du Travail)—communism-oriented trade union
*3. Front National (National Front)—far-right party
*4. Social groups who are frequently doing demonstrations in France

30

Immediate Appearance

Dedicated to Daniel Josien, who succeeded in saving some of them.

—Good morning, Monsieur. Please sit there. Guard, you can remove the handcuffs. But, hey, I recognize you. I have already received you here.

—Yes, Madame Judge.

—Let's look at your files. Effectively, you are a regular. No surprise with a pedigree like yours!

—Pedi—what?

—Pedigree! It a word that assumes all your background in some way. I see there are several arrests for shoplifting, pickpocketing, assaults, resisting arrest, insulting an officer, car theft, and the list goes on!

—Well, um, I don't know.

—Several convictions, probations, and instances of community service also. Those did not calm you down, however!

—Well, um . . .

—So now what is the reason? Ah! This is new! Drug trafficking! You are progressing, I see!

You have been found in possession of drug bags that you were obviously reselling, and you tried to get rid of them when the policemen apprehended you. Do you recognize the facts?

—Ye—no! They fell from my pocket when the cops jacked me!

—So you have holes in your pockets now?

—They shook me and threw me to the ground. Besides, those were not mine!

—Explain yourself! These drugs did not fall down from the sky. From where did they come?

—Yeah, yes. It is a buddy who gave to me a pack for another guy who was going to come and get it later. I swear I had no idea of what they were!

—And you want me to believe such a tale! And that so-called buddy, do you have his name and address?

—Well, um, his name is . . . Louis, I believe. Yes, that's it—Louis! But I have no idea where he is bunking.

—It is amazing how sincere you look! You have nothing else to tell me? That could help your case!

—Well, um, no, Your Honor. Me, I have nothing to do with all of this. I did not know. My word as a man for it. You know, I never touched the stuff!

—Precisely, I know you, and there is a first time for everything. Now, what on earth are we going to do with you? We have nearly tried everything. Alas! People like you are burdening the courts!

—I swear, Your Honor, me—I don't want to be a burden for you. It's because of the cops. They are always on my back!

—If you just mend your way, they will leave you alone and everything will be fine.

—Ah yes, a fine! It's OK with me. I can pay. I have money.

—As I know where this money comes from, I don't think it will be a very effective punishment. What about being put into an apprenticeship so you can learn a real trade and earn your living honestly?

—Uh, if you say so, Madame Judge. I don't mind trying. But what?

—Then the building jobs—for example, woodworking. We actually have a few reserved places for this sort of training. You can become a carpenter, joiner, or cabinet maker. You can build furniture or even become a wood sculptor!

—Yes, but the woodwork, it does get you a lot of splinters in the fingers. You may even lose your sense of touch and cannot even put your hands in your pockets!

—Or, rather, in other people's pockets, perhaps? And what about metalworking? A welder, plumber, or mechanic, perhaps?

—You don't have locksmithing, by chance?

—No! Why?

—I could learn some useful tricks!

—I am afraid of understanding your sudden interest for this job.

—Becoming a mechanic, I like it too, especially a garage mechanic with cars. I love to fiddle with the motors.

—Especially those of other people's cars, I guess! I have to admit that you have a very practical mind. Well, listen—I have an idea, and I shall try to give you one last chance.

—Oh, thank you, Your Honor!

—Here it is. You will exit this room and see my secretary to make an appointment with Monsieur Daniel, who will look after you.

—Monsieur Daniel? Yes, I have understood. I will do what?

—Monsieur Daniel is a special educator working for the tribunal. He has succeeded in reintegrating into society some hard cases like you. He does this by making them participate in nature activities at sea or in the forest or in agriculture. You will see that he is a good man.

—If you say so, Madame Judge! Anyways, I believe I don't have a choice, no?

—No, not really. If not, I shall send you to jail! So here you go now, Monsieur. A good day to you and good luck!

—Thank you, Your Honor. Goodbye, Your Honor. Ah! Excuse me, Your Honor, should I also ask your secretary for an appointment with you?

—No. Why?

—But . . . for the next time?

31

Blasphemies

—Good day, fellas. What do you want?

—Could you please give us some of your time? We would like to discuss with you the words of God.

—He cannot call or come by himself?

—Of course not! We are talking about God, our Redeemer!

—"Redeemer"? I don't know what it is. What is that for? A job? Is that some tax collector or what?

—But no! He is our Savior! The one who sacrificed himself on the cross to save us!

—Ah, good! But me, I have asked for nothing. If it pleased himself to do so, it is his problem.

—You know, the ways of God are mysterious!

—Good for him! How does that matter to me?

—Did you ever think about what will happen after your death or assuring your salvation?

—After my death? That will be a bloody mess. My heirs will fight among themselves. Already they can't see themselves in paint! And about insurance, I have already a life insurance, which costs me an arm and a leg.

—You don't want the kingdom of heaven to belong to you?

—Good to know! Is that for sale?

—But no, you have to win it with your penance and the pardoning of your sins!

—Ah, good! Are there many people on this deal?

—Of course, yes! In fact, everybody is because the leniency of God is infinite!

—If there are so many people, your heaven is some sort of big co-owned property. I don't like co-owned properties. They always bring trouble. And besides that?

—You can redeem yourself by doing good actions. God will give it back a hundredfold!

—Actions that bring you 10,000 percent! This is quite suspicious! Me, I have some that bring only 3 or 5 percent. Or is it that my banker puts the rest in his pocket? There are no smarter thieves than those guys, and the law is with them!

—But no, we are not talking about money but spiritual assets.

—Spiritual? I did not get where it was funny! I must not have the Holy Spirit!

—Alas! Monsieur, I believe that the devil spirit is in you.

—The devil? Hell, if it is in me, I doubt he is so spirited! By the way, tell me—last week, I was visited by some people like you. Some contestants, probably. Some guys with shaved heads. But they—they were offering reincarnation after death. You don't do that, do you?

—No, we have the resurrection after the last judgment.

—A judgment? But I was thinking that we were already forgiven! Is that a double sentence or what? We are not out of the woods yet, considering the number of people and the slowness of justice. Besides that, if you need a lawyer, it will cost you an arm and a leg again. I prefer the reincarnation.

—We also do the reincarnation but only once—after the resurrection!

—But with the others, it is every time. The problem is that they cannot tell you what you will be reincarnated into and you cannot choose! It is unfortunate. It makes the offer less attractive. Me, I am not interested in being reincarnated into a pig and finishing with being eaten in sausages!

—So you see, our offer is competitive!

—It depends. There was also this bearded man who came the other day. He does not want to hear about pigs. On the other hand, he is offering seventy-two virgins! What to do with seventy-two virgins, eh? Some people will be thinking about dirty things. Besides, virgins—they can only be used once, and you already need pretty good health to manage with two or three. Of course, there are some people who will be interested, but me, I am too old for it.

—So, Monsieur, I see that finally—

—Finally, Monsieur, this is not my cup of atheist! Goodbye! My best regards to God!

32

Smartphone

Dedicated to Karin.

—Good day, Mister. You are looking for something?

—I would like some information about phones.

—No problem! We have a large choice of brands and models. It depends on what you want to do and the price you can afford.

—Well, it is for making calls—

—I could have guessed that, but nowadays, phones can do a lot of other useful things, you know. They are smart, and that is why they are called smartphones.

—Ah, good! Show me some and how they work.

—Well, this one, for example, you have, of course, a touch screen, fingerprint sensor, vocal recognition, screen scrolling, access to 4G, processor, 4 GB of RAM, storage up to 132 GB, Wi-Fi and Internet access, Bluetooth connectivity, automatic search, long-life battery—

—Wait, wait! I cannot follow you. I don't understand even half of what you are telling me. Not everybody is an expert in modern technology, you know.

—Yes, I understand, but you are not the only one. It's quite simple, and I am going to explain it to you.

—Quite simple? It's you who say that!

—Well, tell me what you don't understand.

—Well, um, everything! What is 4G? What is Wi-Fi? What is RAM? And this other memory? What is a processor? What is Bluetooth?

—OK, I see. But you will get directions that will explain in detail how you can use the phone.

—Oh dear! That is quite a big manual! It's ten times bigger than the phone. Me, how can I be expected to read all of this? There are plenty of words that I don't even understand. Do you have one in normal English? And this thing here, what is it?

—This a camera. You can shoot all the pictures you want and also videos. It is high-definition! Then you can send them to your friends with your SMS and emails. Look, there are even two cameras so that you can video yourself when you are talking and even see on the screen the person you are talking to.

—These technical progresses are incredible! So everybody can spy on everybody else nowadays? It's crazy!

—And that's not all—far from it! You have also a GPS, which will help you find your way to places.

—Ah yes, that's the thing with a voice telling you to turn right or left and it loses you in the middle of nowhere! City people have landed in my farmyard because of this thingy. They believed they were on the main road!

—Really? That's surprising! Also, if you lose your phone, you can find it with the lost-phone tracker. Of course, you have all the usual features: the calculator, the torch, the choice of alarms, the agenda, the contact list, the call history, the loudspeaker, the calendar, the notebook—

—All in this little thing?

—Yes, and this little "thing," as you say, can also be used to control a lot of home appliances even when you are not there: the lights, the heating, the TV, the security cameras—

—Really? Is there anything that will bring the cows back from the pasture for milking?

—I don't think so, but if your cows were connected, then why not!

—*Wow!* This time, it blows my mind! And what is the price of this marvel?

—Well, it depends on the features, the speed, and the memory, but you must expect to pay at least five hundred euros, but the best go well over a thousand.

—Ah! it is not cheap!

—It is like a car. The price depends on the engine power and the accessories.

—Well, but you know, myself, I mostly drive a tractor, then—

—Then, Monsieur, have you made your choice? I see that you are interested!

—Well, yes, but there is a problem. It is not for me.

—A present, I assume.

—Yes. But the problem is that it is for my old mother—so that we can call her from time to time and check if she is still in this world. She almost never leaves her place and her recliner. And as we used to say, she sees only with one ear and hears only with one eye. So all your tricks—the screen, the buttons, the 4G, the Wi-Fi—she will understand none of it!

—Effectively, that is annoying.

—You don't have one that only does phone calls?

—A phone? Just to talk? No, we don't have that. You will certainly have to wait for the new models! I am sorry, Monsieur.

—There is no harm. I was just getting some information, but I am now going to see how I can get my cows connected, and I shall come back to see you. For sure, one has to go with the progress nowadays.

33

The Word of an Old Man

—Good day, Professor!

—Good day. I understand that you want me to help you with your doctoral thesis?

—Yes. I would be very honored if you accepted.

—Good, and what is the subject you have chosen?

—Well, it's a bit peculiar. My topic is this: "Is bullshit necessary to society?"

—Goodness gracious! This is quite provocative! And what is the point of your research?

—I would like to study and analyze the phenomenon of human stupidity and identify the important role it plays in the proper functioning of our society. The idea behind it is to demonstrate that starting with the recognition that our social systems are all based on the manipulation of individuals by other individuals, the smooth operation of the whole depends on the stupidity level of the ones or of the others!

—But would it not be better to say the same in relation to the intelligence instead of the stupidity of people? That could perhaps be a bit more elegant!

—In theory, maybe yes, because intelligence and stupidity are classically related to each other, albeit as opposites. But practically, it seems evident to me that it is the control and exploitation of stupidity that is at the foundation of the control of all the social groups!

—You are quite affirmative, young man. It seems to me personally that the societies are led by groups of intelligent people!

—Effectively! Or at least, that is what they want us to believe. Indeed, their stupidity is just different from the stupidity of those they are dominating. And this, alas, sometimes has quite-disastrous consequences.

—I am beginning to understand where you are heading with this. But you had better start by presenting a proper definition of what you call bullshit. You can only do this by first giving the definition of *intelligence*— or, better said, the definitions of the different intelligences. We know quite well that there are as many forms of intelligence as there are areas where intelligence can be applied. This does complicate the matter, does it not?

—No, not really—so long as one analyzes correctly the processes, stages, and patterns of intelligence.

—Then, precisely, how do you do that?

—Well, intelligence is first the ability to observe, then to memorize the observations, then to compare the observations and analyze their possible interrelationships, and then, when facing a similar or new situation, being able to use what you have learned and choose the best course of action to take while keeping in mind the fact that one's behavior is always dictated by the very first instinct of survival.

—Let's admit this, while it is a little bit simplistic. But the stupidity, in all of this, where does it come into play?

—Well, it can happen at any stage so long as there is a deficiency or a dysfunction. One can be dumb because they are unable to observe properly. One can be dumb because they are unable to remember what they observed or learned. One can be dumb because they are unable to compare the observations. One can be dumb because they are unable to analyze a situation. One can be dumb because they are unable to recognize a similar or a new situation. One can be dumb because they are unable to find a solution or make a decision! In addition, one can be dumb while letting other people make decisions in their place. One can be dumb by making the wrong choice. One can be dumb—

—Stop! Stop! That's enough! You are scaring me!

—And one can be dumb when one refuses to see that they are dumb and have been doing the wrong thing. This is the most frequent case!

—But in your thesis, you want to extend the matter to the whole of society?

—Absolutely. Because while society can conduct itself as one collective, it quite often reacts as one individual. It can then be manipulated in the same way by controlling the key points: the information control, the communication and expression control, the decision control, the control of the instincts and basic needs, etc.

—Yes, I understand quite well. But this is the ABC of political power— whatever the system—but—

—But if there were no idiots, nothing would operate properly! Imagine if everybody had the same level of intelligence! What a bloody mess it would be! Everybody would want to command everybody else and would want to always be right!

—So your contention is that the idiots are necessary to the functioning of society?

—Without any doubt!

—But you cannot control the idiots solely by controlling their information?

—This is true. You first have to make the idiots feel very happy about themselves and about their situations, especially their material situation. Anyway, they have a natural inclination for that. The idiot wishes to be quiet and cushy: comfort, conformism, conservatism, consummation, conviviality, etc. (*1)

—But we do all, more or less, want the same thing, no? Does that make idiots of us?

—Of course not. We would be really dumb not to enjoy life. But there is something more!

—Ah yes, and what?

—Well, before anything else, you must never forget to tell an idiot that he is intelligent. He will absolutely love to hear this because in his own mind, everyone else is an idiot. If you tell him he is intelligent, he will then believe everything you say.

—I effectively admit that you don't get the same result when you tell an idiot that he is an idiot!

—Now then, Monsieur Professor, my thesis, do you accept to mentor me?

—Young man, you have all my support! And you can take the word of an old idiot!

*1. In French, *con* means "idiot." Therefore, this adds humor to these word combinations.

34

Science without Conscience

Dedicated to Maxime Leluan, a coach if ever there was one.

—Hey, Coach! Can I become a champion?

—You know, everything is possible, but I cannot answer that question now.

—Why not, Coach? You know a lot about champions, no? You have coached many of them.

—That may be true, but I am not a seer, and I don't have a crystal ball.

—But if I do everything you say and I train very hard?

—Then, you will certainly improve your chances, but it may not be enough. In sports, the results are not necessarily in proportion to the efforts.

—That is not fair!

—That may be so, but you should not expect justice in sports—like it is in the rest of society, by the way! It is the strongest, the richest, or the smartest who win—not necessarily the most meritorious or even the most talented.

—But, then, what do you need more to succeed?

—Well, of course, you need to have some potential to start with. Some talent certainly helps. One cannot make a racing horse out of a donkey!

—OK, Coach. You better be tall to play basketball or strong to throw the shot. Everybody knows that. But once we have picked an event that is right for us and are training correctly, why can't we succeed like those guys on TV?

—You know, nothing is won in advance, and one does not know exactly the effects of training. For some people, it works, but for some others, it doesn't. You must also have some luck!

—But, Coach, there are so many super scientific publications about training. You can also get a lot of advice on the net. One should now know what is good or not, no?

—-In fact, no. Indeed, nobody agrees. The scientists contradict one another from one year to the next. And there are little smart-asses making cash with so-called miracle recipes. There are some fashions and fads going on. As soon as somebody is successful and breaks a record, everybody copies him before realizing—too late—that what is good for one is not necessarily good for another.

—But, Coach, there are some who are super strong. We have heard that they take some stuff for it! These products, you must know about them, no?

—That is another story. Sadly, it is true that there are people who are willing to do anything to succeed!

—Then, why don't you use it? We—maybe we would need it. Without it, we might always be beaten.

—Because it is disgusting, dangerous, and dishonest. Don't count on me for that sort of thing. It is doping, and anyways, it is forbidden, or so they say!

—Coach, we believe you, but please explain this better. What do you mean by "so they say"?

—Well, doping is not as simple as it seems. Indeed, there are three dimensions: the scientific, the legal, and the ethical.

—"Scientific"? But, Coach, you just said that the scientists are contradicting one another all the time.

—True, and this concerns doping as well. They don't agree on the substances, their effects, the doses, and the long-term side effects that are discovered too late.

—So it's a bit like the medications that everybody is taking, then?

—Absolutely. In fact, one cannot 100 percent trust the scientists.

—And what about the legal side? There are laws, at least!

—Yes, but the problem is that the laws as to what is allowed and what is not are made after the propositions of the scientists. So, in fact, laws can be based on questionable assessments. One can "charge himself like a mule (*1)" and fit in with the law, and another will get caught after just taking a pill for a headache. There's also the fact that, as it is with many laws, they can be circumvented if the little smart-asses have good lawyers.

—But then, Coach, there is only the ethical left. What is that, the ethical?

—Well, the ethical is about honor, self-esteem, and respecting yourself and others.

—That sounds good! Is that the sporting spirit? So what does the ethical say about doping?

—It says that it all depends on what we have in mind. In fact, we must know if we want to intervene in the natural process artificially or have or not have a doping conduct even if it is legal!

—Please explain it to us, Coach. What is a doping conduct?

—Well, for example, if you drink one coffee, it's OK. It's part of your normal nutrition, but if you take three or four or, worse, pure caffeine to get excited, you have a doping conduct even if you are under the allowed limit.

—So, Coach, it is the intention that counts, no?

—That's pretty much it. You have understood.

—But then, everybody has more a less a doping conduct.

—That's one way to see things, yes!

—Then, Coach, we are not out of the woods with this. The scientists don't know very much, the lawmakers know even less, and the bad conduct continues because nobody really cares much about the ethical. And finally, we are all doped!

—Yes. As you say, we are not done with the problem.

—Yes, but what is to become of us in this mess? And what shall we do now?

—Now? Well, training is finished. The time is up. Come on, let's have a coffee at the bar around the corner to warm ourselves up. It will do us good!

*1. "Loaded like a mule" is a common changing-room phrase that is used to describe doped athletes.

35

Sesame, Open Yourself!

—Allo? Lapage Publishing. Hi! What can we do for you?

—Good morning, Monsieur. I have written a book, and—

—A book? What sort of book?

—Well, they are stories of—

—What kind of stories? A novel? A detective fiction? An autobiography? An erotic novel? There are many kinds!

—Yes, I know, but it's a bit of everything. Indeed, these are memories of—

—Is this your first book?

—Yes! Indeed, I could have written one before but—

—I suppose you would like to publish it?

—Yes, that's correct. Indeed, it is not exactly a novel but some anecdotes that—

—So it is a collection of short stories?

—No, not exactly, but it is related to—

—Is it a book with important content?

—Well, that depends. There are people who like these things and find them important and—

—No, I was talking about the size of the book—the number of words and pages.

—No, it is not very big, but it is quite peculiar. Therefore, I—

—Good! Listen. I don't want to discourage you, but we receive hundreds of propositions like yours every week, and we have to make a choice as to what we are going to publish, especially if the author is unknown.

—I am not known because it is my first book, as I already said.

—Precisely! You know, now, if you want to sell books, you have to be famous before you write them. And in many cases, you don't even have to write anything because somebody will do it for you—a "ghostwriter," as it is called in the business!

—Do you recommend the use of a ghostwriter? Me, I have written it all by myself, and the story has nothing to do with ghosts anyways.

—But are you known somehow? In sports? Politics? You see, at the moment, it is what is selling!

—Known? As I have said, I don't believe I am known. So what am I going to do now?

—OK! You can still send us a few chapters of your manuscript. We shall answer you in time, but don't get any false hopes. Unless we see something exceptional that can sell, you have little chance of getting published. I advise you to send your manuscript to other publishers. One never knows, and you can get lucky—that is, if your book is any good.

—That's fine! I will follow your advice! Goodbye, Mister! Thank you!

—Wait a minute! Before you go, your book, what is it about exactly?

—Well, I was a night manservant at the Ali Baba. I am sure you have heard of it, no? The place where all the stars, politicians, celebrities, and jet-setters stay when they come to town.

—Ah, really? The Ali Baba?

—Yes. I worked there for about forty years, and I can say that I have seen a lot of things! All kinds of things! I am going to tell some of those stories in my book!

—What? Why didn't you tell me that in the first place? Can you come and see me with your manuscript? Let's say tomorrow or the day after tomorrow, if that would work for you. The earlier the better! I am going to prepare a contract. Have you already given thought to a title and a cover?

—No. I have just written about some of the things that I witnessed during all those years.

—Don't worry about that! We shall think about it with our editorial team. Something like *Ali Baba and the Forty Peepers*! No, wait—maybe *My One Thousand and One Nights at the Ali Baba*! Anyways, we shall see. So, Mister, what about tomorrow afternoon? Is that OK with you?

—That's fine! I can come at about 5:00 p.m.

—Good! Just one more thing to consider—I suppose you are going to write under a pseudonym. You know that when one wants to make some money from other people's bed stories, one must take care not to trip over the sheets.

—Of course. I already have one in mind. How about Sesame?

—Great! "Sesame, open yourself!" This is perfect! Goodbye, Mr. Sesame! See you tomorrow!

36

Escapade

Dedicated to my friend Jean Pierre, who, as an official justice locksmith, has seen a number of similar situations.

—Hello, Mister!

—Hello! You are looking for somebody?

—I must see the president! It is important!

—That will be quite difficult at the moment. He is in a meeting. You will have to wait until it is finished.

—A meeting? But we are not at the Chamber here!

—The president has a, let's say, very *private* meeting.

—Listen, I *have* to see him regardless.

—He said that he should not be disturbed under any circumstances, and as a member of his personal protection squad, I must obey his direct orders!

—Be that as it may, it happens that I am the bodyguard of the person who, at this very moment, is meeting with the president and that I am charged with ensuring her protection.

—Ah! Then we are colleagues.

—Exactly, and we must work together because we have a serious situation on our hands—believe me!

—OK, tell me everything.

—Well, it turns out that somebody has gotten wind of this private meeting by the way of an anonymous letter, and it happens that this somebody is extremely concerned and at this very moment is already on his way here. He intends to participate in this meeting in a way that will not be really welcome. You can imagine the situation and the scandal.

—Hell! In other words, the husband is aware and wants to intervene with the game?

—Yes, and game or not, the result is the same. I have been informed that he is coming with a court officer and a locksmith so they can get an official statement.

—Dear, dear, dear! This really does complicate the matters!

—And it gets even more complicated when the cuckolded happens to be one of the chiefs of a political party currently allied with the president to form the actual presidential majority!

—I understand. Ah! And they do themselves no favors, these so-called political friends. So it is a little bomb that we have to defuse. If the scandal bursts out, the political alliance will fall apart, and the government will topple. We must act quickly! What do you propose we do? If this other guy is already on his way with his bailiff, we don't have much time.

—Well, here is my plan: We discreetly exfiltrate the wench, then we get the president to go back just as he came—incognito on his scooter.

—That seems simple enough. OK, let's go wake them up! But this time, they will not get coffee and croissants! Then you and I will each deal with our respective employer. No muss, no fuss, and a clean place. We will stay connected via radio in case of trouble. Come on, GO!

—Allo! Colleague? Here is all clear. We got the baby out in an unmarked vehicle without any problem. No newspaper guys around. Even better, in case the husband shows up with his lawman, I have arranged for a female member of our security squad to create some confusion by playing the role of the lass. If we have to play a bit of vaudeville, then let's have a bit of fun! And you, has everything gone like clockwork?

—Clockwork? No. In fact, we came very close to disaster. Can you believe that the president had left his scooter in the doorway with the keys on the contact? And it did not miss to happen! His scooter was stolen!

—That cannot be true! This one, he never misses a crap! Then, what did you do? I guess It was out of the question to use an official vehicle to repatriate him with all these newspapermen like vultures on the lookout.

—Yes, so in urgency, we requisitioned the scooter of a guy passing by, and we sent our man incognito just before the other idiot arrived with his justice officer and the locksmith!

—Phew! That was a close one! I bet the fellow must have made a weird face when he saw the plonk instead of his sweet and tender!

—Yes! Everybody was laughing behind his back!

—I can't help thinking about the keys that were taken with the president's scooter. I hope the key of our nuclear strike force was not in the set.

—No, I don't think—I hope not!

—What a happy, bloody mess, this republic, though!

—Yes. You certainly got that right!

*1. *Vaudeville*—a type of entertainment featuring a mixture of burlesque comedy, song, and dance.

37

High School Diploma on Sale

—Monsieur Education Commissioner, here is the report on the high school diploma examination of your district.

—Very good! That has come through quickly. Tell me orally the main points.

—So, well, this year, we have registered a 99.9 percent success rate!

—That is remarkable, indeed. The ministry will be satisfied. But how have you managed to achieve this result?

—Teamwork, Monsieur Commissioner. The inspectors, the markers, the statistics service—everybody has been doing their best.

—But what about the candidates?

—Bof! The candidates—they were no better than usual and probably even worse!

—Then I compliment you. But what about this missing 0.1 percent? Did you find who's responsible?

—Yes! We conducted an inquiry, and it seems that some of the candidates refused to give their examination papers.

—What do you mean "refused"?

—Yes, they said we could go to hell with our stupid examination and they had better things to do than waste their time with this comedy!

—These young people seem to be very unaware and unconcerned about their future!

—Not necessarily. It happens that some of them are already heading start-up businesses with budgets of more than a million dollars. They say they expect no benefit from this piece of paper that we try to force them to obtain.

—Well, if they are happy with that, we cannot blame them. Besides this, were there any other incidents that we had to deal with?

—Not many. A cleaning woman discovered the answer schedule of the C series in a trash can of the rectorate!

—And?

—And she used them and passed the exam with distinction! We thought it was wiser not to give too much publicity to this affair, and we validated the result.

—Of course, I understand. What else?

—Well, there was a marker who posted a video of himself on Facebook to show his marking method. He stood at the top of some stairs and threw the papers down. They more or less fell according to the weight and the number of pages. Then he picked them up and gave them a mark according to the step they landed on. The best marks were given to those that landed the furthest down the stairs (*1)!

—But this is unspeakable! Did we find this person?

—Yes, but first, we had this video deleted!

—We must put him in front of a disciplinary board for grave professional misconduct!

—That may prove difficult!

—Why so?

—It happens that he is one of our best markers. His marks statistically conform perfectly with the instructions, and he has been recently nominated for the Academic Palms Award (*2)!

—So you are saying that we can do nothing?

—Well, maybe we should do nothing. Because in the end, he did not do anything wrong as everybody succeeded.

—This damned examination should be sorted out!

—Yes. People are thinking about it, and the ministry experts are working on a new version—a Bac video game (*3). A candidate could use their game console to sit and pass their exam if they succeed to achieve a course and beat the villains trying to prevent them from achieving their examination. There will, of course, be several levels in the game to allow candidates to get merits and distinctions!

—I am stunned! Oh dear! It's good that I'm retiring soon and will no longer be an accomplice to this poor comedy!

*1. Authentic!
*2. Academic Palms is a specific distinction in the French educational system.
*3. Bac, or Baccalaureat, is the name of the final high school diploma in France.

38

The Spirit of the Laws

—Hey! What happened to you? Your cheek is all red!

—It's my mom. She gave me a slap in the face!

—Dear! She certainly connected! What did you do?

—I was being insolent with her.

—Hey! That may be so, but she has no right to do that, you know!

—No? Why not?

—Because there is a new law about that. Spanking, slapping, kicking up the arse—parents cannot do those things anymore.

—And who churned out this law?

—The government, of course.

—The government? They would do better with looking after their own bums than other people's bums, if you ask me.

—Yeah! But now, if you want, you can complain to the police.

—Are you nuts or what? I am not going to report my parents for a smack that I deserved. If I did that—hello! Just imagine the atmosphere of the house when I went back! They would kick me out. And I could expect that this time, it would be my father who would beat my brains out. And as he was a former rugby scrum half, he could kick your ass from all possible positions! Did the idiots who made that law think about the consequences?

—Is your father a bully?

—Not at all. We get along quite well. It's only when I do something really bad that he talks to me with his size 12 boot. But really, that only happens when I push things a bit too far. In fact, he even told me that he was going to teach me the technique. He said, "You see, my boy, you are like me when I was your age—a tough, pigheaded fella. I was on the receiving end of your grandfather's boot on many occasions, but I can never thank him enough. It helped me make my way in life!"

—Ah yes! And what is your dad doing with his life?

—He's a street cleaner. Why?

—For sure he has made his way! Well cleaned! Ha ha!

—You can talk! And what is your father doing? Just fucking around and cashing the allowances!

—So what? It is not against the law!

—By the way, what are you doing here with that canister?

—It's petrol. Tonight, we are going to have a little party with the buddies—set two or three cars afire. You want to come? It is fun!

—No! And if you think you know so much about our laws, you should know that there are laws about this sort of fun as well, no?

—Yeah! But we have the right to have some fun from time to time after all! And because we are teenagers, even the cops cannot touch us! Do you see the old Peugeot parked over there?

—Yes, I do.

—Well, we are going to have fun with that old rusty bucket, and the owner can buy himself a new one with the insurance money! Good, eh?

—Hey! What are you doing? Are you crazy? Ouch! Argh! You bastard! Motherfucker! Why did you kick me in the balls? Ouch! Damn! It hurts!

—You idiot! That old Peugeot is my dad's car, and the kick in the balls is on his behalf. It's just unfortunate that I don't yet have all his technique!

—You son of a bitch! You took me by surprise!

—Maybe, but now you are in the loop. And make sure you leave the Peugeot alone, OK? Otherwise, when I have finished with you, you will have balls so dented that no one could even play petanque with them! Seeing as you know the laws so well, you can still complain to the cops, if you want. They may even die laughing!

39

The World Is a Sustainable Shit Ball

Dedicated to Michel de Montaigne (*1).

—Good morning, Monsieur Chief Executive Officer. I have brought you the report you requested about the restructuring plan of our company.

—Good morning, Monsieur Duchemin. Very good. Let's have a look. Hmm. Yes, well, effectively, it looks very comprehensive. In short, can you give me your concluding observations and recommendations?

—Yes, Monsieur. The first thing we must note is that our company is healthy and well managed.

—Good news! But I was already aware of that.

—Certainly, but as health is the state that precedes illness, the state of good health of our company is, in fact, worrisome.

—How so? Explain yourself!

—Yes, in the commercial context, as in many others, those who do not progress, regress! We must ensure that we continue to develop ourselves so we can cope with the always-growing concurrence.

—It is a headlong flight that you are proposing, no? But is there not a risk? This makes me think of the fable of the Frog and the Ox (*2). You know it, I suppose?

—Yes, but there are also other alternatives, which I have recommended in my study!

—Keep going.

—Well, we will have to reduce our production costs, especially the personnel costs.

—Which means?

—That we part with about two hundred staff and redistribute the tasks between the others.

—So you think we should produce two hundred jobless people! And what will become of them?

—No, not two hundred jobless people. We can conceal the fact, as usual, with the employment center, training courses, early retirements, transfers, negotiated departures, etc.

—But a lot of them will fall by the wayside. We will surely have the trade unions on our back!

—We can always deal with them. We can play give-and-take and portray ourselves as the saviors of the remaining jobs. It's all about compromises!

—You are talking so easily about this! And the rest of your propositions, what are they?

—Well, at some stage in the future, our company will have to seriously think about relocating our production. We have the choice between Asia and Eastern Europe. We made a projection on the computer. It shows that after only two years of reinvestments and transfers, we should be able to compensate for the costs of the operation and start making money again.

—The costs of the operation? But who would bear the brunt of this story? More jobless people?

—It is quite probable, but you will have the support of the shareholders!

—Well, if I have understood you correctly, you are saying that we are healthy, but to not become ill, we have to either get bigger with a risk of losing our authenticity or get smaller, which will require us getting rid of many staff or diluting ourselves through globalization and doing anything with anybody. Did I understand that right?

—That's about the picture of it, Monsieur CEO, in simple terms!

—Well, Monsieur Duchemin, I am going to put something else in simple terms. First, I thank you for your work on this study—of which I reckon the seriousness, considering the factors that you have considered.

—Ah, thank you, Monsieur CEO.

—But alas, as it is common with this type of study made by people like you, there is a factor that you have completely overlooked, and this is, for me, the most important: it is the human factor!

—How is that so? Monsieur CEO, on the contrary—

—Yes, I see you are talking in terms of market shares, productivity, benefits, investments, state-of-the-art developments, reduction of expenses, etc. It is the language of your world and of our actual world. On the other hand, it happens that I personally belong to an endangered species in this world.

—But, Monsieur CEO, I—

—It also happens that I still own the controlling interest of this company, which I inherited from my family. This company was created by my great-grandfather with a few workers, and I, the fourth-generation owner, have received this responsibility from my father. I have maintained it as well as I could with the same spirit. I know personally most of the workers. They are happy to see me and come to shake my hand. They put their confidence in me. How could you imagine for even one second that, to make more money, I would put any of these good people out of work? I would not even dare to meet their eyes!

—But you are not obliged to see them in person.

—But who do you believe I am? One of those criminal bosses who got away with golden parachutes?

—Monsieur, I would not permit myself to think of such a thing, but one has to make some decisions!

—Don't worry about that. I can make decisions. Well, if I have to cut staff, you will have to give me a list of 199 people to lay off.

—But why 199? I believe I said 200.

—No, it is 199 because you will put your name at the top of the list.

—WHAT? Monsieur CEO! But I have done my work correctly. I cannot understand this. This is terrible and unexpected and—

—Alas, yes, Monsieur Duchemin, it's terrible indeed. I am sorry.

—But what will become of me?

—Ah, well, as you suggested earlier—employment center, training courses, early retirements, etc. You know those better than me.

—Oh dear!

—OK. Now, come on. Get over it. Indeed, it was a joke—a bad joke, I must admit. But you needed it. You will not be laid off, I assure you. On the contrary, I am going to give you another job—one that better fits your capacities because you are serious and reliable in everything you do. But

I hope that you will now understand the importance of the human factor and learn to see things from another perspective.

—Ah, Monsieur CEO, I have not yet recovered. You gave me such a shock!

—It's nothing. It will go away. Now listen to me. Here are my decisions: first, be clear that we are not going to bite more than we can chew and will certainly not be buying rotten businesses that you have to lift back up. On the contrary, we will reinforce our image and our position in the market and concentrate our efforts on what has made us a success. Our priority will be to retain our customers instead of running around the world to get new ones who will turn their backs on us at the first opportunity.

—I understand, Monsieur CEO.

—Then, we will not dismiss anybody, including you. Instead, we shall make a force out of the human factor. Value, secure, and look after ALL our collaborators—from the most modest bolt clamper to the little computer genius. They must be proud to work for us, and believe me, they already are.

—Yes, for sure it sounds good, but what about profitability?

—I will get to that soon. But first, understand that there is no question about relocating anything. Quite the opposite, we will further strengthen the brand image of the products we make in OUR country with OUR resources and OUR know-how and prioritize our internal market. This is a lot safer than depending on the goodwill of hypothetical and fluctuating exterior markets and being at the mercy of capricious international contexts.

—I see that, Monsieur CEO, but how do we do all of this practically and make it work?

—Well, for a start, we shall conduct a very strict internal review—post by post—and see what we can improve and where we can eliminate wastes of time and raw material. See, for example, the packaging and distribution circuits. Don't tell me that we need three different types of packaging for the same product. That is just stupid.

—But the customers are very sensitive to the packaging. It needs to be attractive for them!

—Yes, but the price and the quality are also attractive for our true customers. I am going to put you in charge of this review, and I will give you two collaborators: one will be an experienced field worker, and the other will be a young guy who is an expert in the latest technologies and who will, I'm sure, bring lots of fresh ideas. Now get on with your new assignment and come back to see me in a fortnight. Then we will consider which suggestions we can implement immediately and which we shall introduce progressively. You will see that our production costs will fall without the reduction of our staff!

—Well, Monsieur CEO, that will be done.

—I am counting on you, and remember, what matters to me is not the money we are making but what is in the eyes of my employees and the warmth of their handshakes. Now go, Monsieur Duchemin. There is work to be done. Goodbye, Monsieur Duchemin.

—Goodbye, Monsieur CEO. You have convinced me, and . . .

—And?

—And please allow me to shake your hand!

—My pleasure, Monsieur Duchemin! My pleasure!

1. Michel de Montaigne, French philosopher (1533–1592). The original quote is "Le monde n'est qu'une branloire perenne."
2. One of Aesop's fables in which a frog tries to inflate itself to the size of an ox but bursts in the attempt.

40

Gone with the Wind

—Well, everybody is here? Yes? Sergeant! You can proceed.

—Thank you, sir. Men, your platoon has been chosen to perform a survival exercise in extreme conditions. The code name of the operation is Boomerang. Tonight at 2300, you will embark in a light plane from the special operation's service that will drop you at a secret location in the nearby mountain range. You will not have any orientation instrument, water, food, or radio. Winter battle dress with weapons and equipment. At this time of the year, the temperature drops well below zero on this high mountain plateau. You will have only one survival blanket for every two members. No possibility to light a fire, and only one torch for the whole platoon. Take care. It can last for only half an hour if it is used continuously. Those are the general conditions. Have you taken notes?

—Yes, Chief!

—Now, the suite of the mission: After taking off, the plane will proceed directly toward the operational zone. The windows will be blackened to prevent any possible visual orientation with the ground. When you are over the drop zone, the plane will make several circles to disorient you even more before dropping you at an altitude of five hundred meters from the ground. Estimated drop time is 2330. There will be a blue beacon on the ground. It will mark the center of the zone, and it is to be the meeting point. This beacon will shut down automatically at 2345. If you miss it, you will be in big trouble. There's no need for me to draw you a picture of that!

—And then, Serg?

—After the drop, land as close as you can to the beacon. Recover your parachutes. Rally together. Discuss the situation and decide on the action you will take. You have two choices: stay in that spot, survive the night, and at daybreak, orientate yourselves. If you pick this option, you will have to hurry as you will have only four hours left to reach your objective. Or you can decide to take a night march in rugged terrain if you think you know the direction you have to take. Your objective is to get back to the base with the full platoon and all your weapons and equipment before 1200. This gives you twelve hours to cover a distance of twenty-five kilometers as the crow flies. The only thing I can tell you is that the location of the base relative to the drop zone is south-southeast. You will have the opportunity to look at the area map for five minutes. But the map will not be oriented and will have no place-names. A red cross will mark the objective, but the starting point will not be marked. You will just get a general idea of the profile of the area. Any questions?

—Yes, Serg! What if something goes wrong? An accident can always happen. Is there something planned?

—First, you will have to manage the problem by yourselves and try to pull through. Only in the case of a life-threatening situation can you use a rescue buoy. It is in the sealed emergency kit and has an electronic locator system that you can trigger to call for help. We shall have a Puma (*1) on alert, and within thirty minutes, we can arrive at the zone. But using the emergency kit will result in the failure of the mission. Any other questions?

—No, Serg!

—Ah, yes! I had nearly forgotten it. I am not coming with you as I have already done this mission before, and that would distort the game. It is Corporal Dujardin who will ensure the command of the platoon, but we are expecting from you a high degree of teamwork and the pooling of your resources.

—Got it, Serg!

—Well, go now and prepare yourselves. By 2200, inspection of men and equipment. By 2215, boarding of the VTL (*2), which will take you to the air base. By 2240, arrival at the air base and immediate transfer to the plane. By 2245, takeoff. You are lucky—the weather forecast is not too bad: very cold in the middle of the night and cloudy without rain but some snowflakes in altitude. Starting now, it is strictly forbidden to communicate with the outside—that means that you can't talk with anyone who is not in this room. Of course, you are not allowed to leave your barracks. Understood? Captain, would you like to add anything?

—No, Sergeant. This is quite clear. Good luck, everybody. You are dismissed!

—Good morning, Serg! Ah, breakfast! Bon appétit!

—WHAT? What the hell are you doing here? Right now, you should be trudging with the others of your platoon in the mountain. Why did you not go?

—But, Serg, we have gone, and we are already back!

—But where have you been?

—We have been on the mission, Serg. We followed the program!

—But at this time of the day, you should be lost up there on the plateau, freezing your balls off and hoping to be fished out.

—But, Serg, we were in a hurry to come back and impatient to see you!

—Don't take me for a fool, Corporal! Just tell me the truth, please!

—But, Serg, it is the truth! The plane dropped us. We saw the blue beacon. Everybody landed safely. We got together at the meeting point, and we decided to risk a night march.

—But that was the most risky choice. How did you know the direction to go?

—Well, we have a guy in the platoon, Mathurin, who apparently, before joining the army, was something of a poacher in his village. He said that we had to climb up the plateau instead of heading down—what everybody else was instinctively inclined to do. He said it was a trap to lead us astray. He was so sure about it that he was ready to bet a week of his pay if he was wrong. So we listened to him and started climbing in single file with Mathurin at the front with our one torch. It was a dark night, so we tied our belts together to make something like a climbing rope in order to not get separated. It was Lavoriaz who got that idea. He was born in the Savoy mountains. We progressed slowly.

—And you did not rest?

—We did. Every forty-five minutes, we had a short break, and to make sure that we did not freeze, we used the South Pole's penguins' tactic. We stood together in a tight group to warm ourselves. We had our backs toward the outside and took turns in being in the inside.

—Very smart, that, and then?

—We tied our four survival blankets together to build a sort of tent roof under which the eight of us packed together. I cannot say that we were warm, but we could have a short rest and recover a bit before moving again.

—Great idea, and then?

—Well, once we had gone over the pass, it was all downhill. We could even see the lights of the city on the horizon. We found a forest path and came across an isolated farm where a peasant was taking out his cows. He got a bit afraid when he saw us coming out of the woods with our camouflage masks and our weapons, but once he realized who we were, he invited us for a round of hot coffee. Lachaume, who was a farmer himself in Normandy, helped him milk his beasts, and to thank us, the old fellow took us all in his tractor trailer down to the village.

—You have been lucky!

—Possibly! But the people around there, they were more or less involved in the maquis resistance (*3) during the last war, and they know what it means to survive in the mountain in winter. In fact, our old chap said that when he saw us, we reminded him of the good old days and that he was nearly expecting to hear again a burst of machine-gun fire coming from the bush!

—And finally?

—Finally, it was the milkman who collected us at the village after we bought him a couple of drinks. He took us close to the base, and here we are, Serg—all of us—with weapons and equipment!

—That will do, Corporal Dujardin. But come with me to see the captain. We shall have to hear what he thinks about all of this.

—Yes, Sergeant!

—Captain, the Boomerang team is back.

—Yes, I know.

—But, sir, how could you know that already? They have only just reported in.

—Yes, Sergeant. We took the precaution of hiding an electronic bug in their equipment, and the gadget allowed us to follow them step-by-step on our computer screens.

—Wow! That's something! So you already know everything?

—Not the details, but we could guess what was going on.

—Captain, this is Corporal Dujardin—in case you want to ask him any questions.

—Good idea. He can tell us his story. They have done very well indeed. But I have only one question to ask him at this stage: Well, Dujardin, tell me—how did you pick the right direction to go after the platoon had regrouped on the plateau?

—It was that bloody Mathurin, the former poacher, sir! It came down to betting—a week of our pay. And that smart-ass, he is counting his money now!

—But how did he know? Did you ask him about his trick?

—He said, "THE WIND!"

—The wind?

—Yes, and he even added, "There is no wind in their f—— computers or on their bloody maps, and the bloody army will still need people like me!"

—Explain yourself!

139

—Well, he explained that when we boarded the plane at the air base, the wind was coming from the north-northwest. You could feel it easily. The plane took off while facing the wind, as they usually do, and then kept going in that direction. Then, at the time of the drop-off, the two circles that the plane made in order to disorientate us were pretty much useless because the machine had to face the wind again anyway before we would jump out. Therefore, it was heading north-northwest again. Once we were on the ground, we only had to keep the wind at our backs to walk south-southeast—toward our objective. Mathurin said that even the stupidest poacher would know that the first thing you do to find your way and hunt successfully is to feel the wind!

—Thank you, Corporal. That will do. You are dismissed. Sergeant? We shall have a general debriefing about this operation later.

—The wind! Damn the wind! That will not make me look very smart when I shall have to explain to the colonel that despite all our technology, we have been made a fool of by a simple village poacher!

*1. Puma—French army helicopter
*2. VTL—French army troop light carrier
*3. *Maquis* were resistance pockets of guerrillas that fought against the Germans during WWII. The most famous was the one in the Alpen, on the Vercors plateau.

41

Free-Exchange Zone

—Hey! You there! Don't move! You're not from around here?

—No.

—Then what the hell are ya mucking around here for? We did not ask ya to come! We don't like tourists!

—I came to visit my auntie who lives in this suburb.

—Ah, Mister has an auntie. A white ass like ya'self?

—Well—

—Here, we have no white asses anymore. You're at the wrong place, bro!

—OK, I—

—Hey, stop! Don't go! We are not done yet. Come on, empty ya pockets!

—But why? I—

—Fuck off! Empty ya pockets, I said!

—But I don't understand! I—

—Hey, if ya don't understand, my buddies over there will help ya figure it out faster. Isn't that right, y'all? Well, that's better. I see ya just needed to be asked nicely. It's so much easier. Let's have a look—only twenty euros! Are you sure ya don't have more hidden?

—No, it is all that I have!

—Ah! But this is a lot better! What a pretty smartphone! Who'd ya steal this from?

—I did not steal it! I bought it!

—This is getting better and better! Mr. Tourist has only got twenty euros in his pocket but is fucking around with the latest smartphone. Me, I think ya have a filthy spy face. An't that true, buddies?

—Yeah! Here, we don't do for the little snoopers!

—OK. Give me that phone.

—But, no . . . I—

—Give it to me, I tell you! Great! How convenient! It's my favorite brand. Well, give me the password now. That will save us time.

—But you don't have the right. I—

—Give me the password, I said! I am beginning to get tired of having to say everything twice. Are ya deaf or are ya dumb or what?

—But it is MY phone. It's personal—

—It WAS your phone, bro! Hey, see here. Who is this pretty little chick on your screen saver? Wow, I bet she's a little sweetie babe. Ah, Mr. Tourist is a lucky fella! Don't say that she came with ya? Where is she?

—No, I am only by myself, I swear.

—Bad luck! We could have shared. You know, we here, we are for sharing and free exchange. Ah, I could even have swapped her for ya phone. See, we are not as bad as we look! Well, now hit the road!

—But my phone?

—Shove it, I said! Don't force me to repeat myself again, or I could change my mind. I am in a good mood today, but don't push your luck too far. Ain't that right, buddies?

—So they let you go?

—Yes, Constable.

—You were lucky! Usually, it does not end so well. So what do you want to do now?

—Well, the police can find them, no?

—Yes. We could do that easily. We do know them quite well.

—So what are you going to do?

—Nothing! We are not going to risk starting a riot to recover a phone. That's it! If you want, you can make a written declaration. We do have forms for this.

—And if I fill out a form, what will it change?

—Nothing! We put it there in the cupboard with all the others.

—And then?

—And then? Nothing!

—And if they had beaten me?

—Well, in that case, we would make a record of the incident.

—Ah, good. And the record, it goes where?

—Yeah, same place—in the cupboard!

—And if they had injured me or even worse?

—Then we would prepare a police report!

—Ah, at least! And the report, where does it go?

—Where do you think? In the cupboard, as usual. What else would you want us to do?

—I don't know exactly, but you could alert your superiors, for example!

—Our superiors know perfectly well about this situation.

—Then what?

—Consider that we are hardly a dozen cops in this police station and that there are hundreds of them in that suburb. Some of them even have weapons. Let's be happy that they are not attacking us. So you see, it is quite simple!

—So you are saying that the police cannot arrest the rabble these days?

—No. That was good for your dad's police! Another epoch—a long time ago!

—A long time ago?

—Yes, a very long time—well before we had smartphones!

42

It Is Disturbing!

—Good day, Madame! What can I do for you?

—It is my car. It is making a curious noise. Could you check what it is?

—Certainly. But what sort of noise? A metallic noise?

—Yes, but it is difficult to describe. It could be a squeaking or a whistling or maybe a clicking.

—And from what part of the car does it come from?

—I don't know. Underneath or maybe at the front. What do you think it could be?

—It is disturbing, but we are going to check that now. Here. Wait for me to open the hood. Good. Now start the motor! Hmm. Hmm. I don't hear anything unusual coming from the motor. It is running fine. Give some gas. OK, you can stop it.

—So what now?

—Nothing. It is disturbing. We'll have to go for a road test. Let's do it now. You will drive, and I will listen. There. Go. Take the road on the left. That's good. Accelerate. Good! Well, now brake. OK, that's good! Now put it in neutral and freewheel down the hill. Good. Do you hear something?

—Well, no, not really. Perhaps . . . yes, there—at the front—behind the dashboard or under. Listen. It seems there is something bizarre—like a sizzling in the background. Do you hear it?

—It's possible. This sizzling in the background is indeed quite bizarre. To be sure, we will have to check under the car. We will need to put it on the hoist. Turn here now so we can go back to the garage.

—So now, what do you suspect? Is it serious?

—I don't know. There are many possible reasons: the rockers, the bearings, the exhaust, the silent blocks, the steering, the brake pads, the valves, and the camshaft. In all cases, it is disturbing! By the way, you are aware that your car is not very young?

—No, but I never had any problem until now. I do not drive very much, you know!

—Yes, but cars age as much in the garage as they do on the road, you know. It happens quite often with the older cars: everything runs fine for years, and then suddenly, without any obvious reason, you have one problem after another. Besides, with these old models, the parts are getting hard to find.

—And do you think I can still drive my car for some time to come?

—I don't know. It could just give up at any moment!

—It is disturbing. What would you advise me to do?

—Well, it is up to you. But maybe it is time to move to something more modern and reliable. We have some models that are quite affordable and perform well. Then, with the warranty you get with a newer car, you should have no issues for quite some time!

—Yes, you are right, but it breaks my heart to separate from this one.

—I understand. One can get quite attached to a machine. To help things, we could make you a good trade-in offer if your old car passes the technical inspection.

—Ah, how much?

—Hmm . . . because it's you, maybe three thousand! There is the risk that your old car will not be easy to resell even if we can overhaul it and don't get caught by hidden costs!

—Pfou! Three thousand—that is not much!

—I know, but you can do what you want. It is the market that sets the price. People want to buy new, and at the moment, prices for secondhand cars are fairly low. So what are you thinking of doing?

—I don't know. All of this comes as a complete surprise!

—Yes, and that's why it could be a good idea to protect yourself from other surprises as this is now quite disturbing.

—Do you believe so?

—It's up to you to decide, but if it were me . . . well, I am not in your position, of course. OK, if you decide now, we may even be able to get you a good payment plan for a new vehicle with a five-year warranty, including labor and parts.

—Ah, yes. Good. OK, I will do it. I will leave you this one as a trade-in. Let's go now and have a look at your new models.

—Allo! Julien?

—Hey, Jean Claude! It's you? Hi! How are you doing?

—Yeah! Quite fine! Tell me, are you still searching for a secondhand Spitfire in good condition?

—Yep!

—Well, old chap, I've got a superb one. Well-maintained inside and out. Not many kilometers on the clock despite its age. Mechanically flawless. Runs like a dream! You will see!

—And how much do you want for it?

—Six thousand!

—You crook! I know you, but we shall see. Wait for me. I am coming now to see this marvel!

—OK! For you, I will wait before putting it in the showroom. You can take it for a test drive. You will not be disappointed. You will see that it's a jewel!

—And if you turn the correct knob to stop the sizzling of the radio, there won't be any noise!

43

Beer under Pressure!

—Sorry, Monsieur. Excuse me.

—Yes?

—Would you like to move from your place and finish your meal in the airport's food hall?

—Not really. Why? I am fine here, and I am not done with the food tray that I bought at your counter.

—Yes, Monsieur, but you bought a draft beer at another nearby counter, and you are drinking it with your meal in our customer area.

—So what? As far as I am aware, this is not forbidden. In this country, it is a common practice for people to bring their own alcoholic drinks. In the food hall, everybody buys food and drinks here and there and sit themselves wherever they want to enjoy their meals.

—Yes, but some of our customers are disturbed, and they have complained.

—Ah? This is something! And I am afraid to guess what sort of customers you are talking about.

—Yes, Monsieur. Please believe that I am very sorry.

—Excuse me, Miss. What country are we in?

—Australia, Monsieur. Why?

—Because as far as I know, the rules of this country apply to this very spot. And the rules also apply to the public zone of this international airport as well. It is not a place that is under the rule of any religion. There are special areas reserved for religious activities and observances.

—Monsieur, I understand, but you are bothering our customers. You have to leave this area. You can sit down there—outside our area.

—I shall do nothing of the sort and have no intention of moving even one inch. If seeing me troubles them, they need only look the other way. That is what I am doing myself as far they are concerned! And if they fancy getting down on all fours to do their prayer, I don't give a damn so long as they don't force me to do the same. Me, I am simply drinking my beer in peace, and I will not force anybody to do like me.

—Monsieur, I am afraid that I will have to refer this situation to our manager.

—Do as you please, and while you are at it, can you also suggest that he call the airport police and ask them to kick me out? I am pretty sure that they will be delighted to remind him of the laws of this country!

—Monsieur?
—Yes, Miss?
—Monsieur, you can finish your meal at your convenience. The manager would like you to accept our apologies. It was a misunderstanding.
—A misunderstanding! Really? I wish I could believe you.
—Do you need anything else, Monsieur?
—No, thank you. I am fine. Ah yes. Miss, please!
—Yes, sir?

—This Indonesian bami is delicious. I would have enjoyed the chance to have some more one day, but I am afraid that, that is unlikely as I will not come back, and I am not going to recommend this place to my friends.

(*) Absolutely authentic—Sydney Airport (2006)

44

Without the Knowledge of My Own Free Will (*1)

Dedicated to Louis PALLURE

—Are you Monsieur Favier?

—Yes, I am!

—You are here because of a persisting pain in your belly?

—That is right.

—And, in fact, you had a bowel surgery in this hospital three weeks ago, which was performed by Professor Lahernie.

—Exactly.

—And since then, it is even more painful?

—Yes! It hurts when I move and also when I am sitting or lying.

—Well, that is no surprise. You can even call yourself lucky that it has not been worse than that!

—How is it lucky?

—Yes! We have received the results of the scan you had earlier today.

—And?

—Well, the scan clearly suggests the presence of a foreign object in your belly. It is believed to be a hemostatic clip!

—A what clip?

—Hemostatic! It is a clip that is used during the surgical procedure to close off the blood vessels. It was forgotten there by the surgeon and the medical team. This is an extremely rare case, but it does happen sometimes.

—And it had to happen to me!

—You know, the medical teams are overworked and often have to operate with urgency and in a hurry. Error is human, alas!

—And is that all that he has forgotten, this surgeon of yours? I don't know. Maybe he left his denture? Or his glasses? It's more likely to be his glasses, by the way, which would at least explain why he did not see the clip!

—Come on, come on! Don't mock him. We are going to put things right.

—So that means that I have to go under the knife again?

—Yes, and as soon as tomorrow. We will admit you shortly so you can be prepped and will be ready first thing in the morning.

—Good, and I hope that they will tidy up properly after their work this time!

—Of course! Everything will be fine. You can rely on us. Well, meanwhile, you will have to go to the hospital administration to sort out a few details. You better go now, Monsieur. They have been told that you are coming.

—Are you Monsieur Favier?

—Yes, I am.

—Well, we have to finalize some administrative details for your surgery tomorrow morning, plus we also need to settle matters related to the surgery you had three weeks ago.

—Ah? What matters?

—Well, after that surgery, you took some chirurgic equipment away with you.

—But it was without the knowledge of my free will (*1), for sure!

—Maybe so, but we are held accountable for this equipment, and you had no authorization!

—WHAT!

—Yes, and so far, this equipment has not been returned or paid for.

—WHAT? Do you realize what you are talking about? For the last three weeks, I have been running around with one of your thingies—which you forgot—inside my belly, and you are virtually accusing me of stealing it! I must be dreaming!

—But you left the hospital with it. Therefore, it must appear on the surgery's invoice. I have revised it, and you now owe us 22.45 euros!

—But as I have to undergo surgery again tomorrow, you will be able to recover your bloody clip, no? So what is this administrative circus for?

—This is not a circus, Monsieur! Please, moderate your language. I am doing my job—that's all! Now, if we effectively recover this equipment, that will change the billing. In fact, it will then become a hire—of course, under the condition that the material is returned undamaged. In that case, you will owe us—let's calculate that—one euro per day for twenty-one days . . . that will amount to twenty-one euros, plus taxes.

—At this price, it's cheap! I might as well keep it as a souvenir!

—Why not, Monsieur? That could be a funny and original idea. Should I assume that you now wish to keep it? Then I can prepare your invoice accordingly.

—You would not prefer to wait for tomorrow? You don't know if they will forget something else behind my liver or in the folds of my intestines. You could make me a deal!

—Ah, Monsieur, I see that you take it with humor. I wish you good luck for tomorrow and hope that everything goes well this time and without additional costs.

—Thank you! I do hope so too. And I hope your gut choppers have found another place to store their tools!

*1. Quote from Richard Virenque, a French cyclist champion, who said it when he was convicted of a doping offense.

45

A Bountiful Sport

—Ah, good morning, Monsieur. I see that you have been able to free yourself from other commitments. I am delighted that you can join us today. Please come, and I will introduce you to the other hunters. They are having a solid breakfast before we start, as is traditional. We, the hunters, are here to maintain the traditions. Isn't that so?

—Certainly! But actually, you know, for me, it is my first time!

—Yes, I know. His Lordship informed me when he did the invitations. Don't worry. It is all quite convivial, and everything will be fine, you will see. You will be in excellent company.

—I have no doubt about that. How many of us are here today?

—About thirty guns, not counting the beaters, the wardens, and the hounds. Yes, that's a lot of people. But thinking of it, am I correct to assume that you have no equipment?

—Pretty much. I have only these boots and a hunting vest that I bought yesterday.

—That will do very well, and you don't have a gun?

—No.

—Have you at least been hunting or shooting before?

—Honestly, no! The only shooting I have done was at cardboard targets at the village fair with my mates!

—OK, we shall work with that. Of course, we have everything we need for our one-day guests. Here, on this rack, you have the choice. I would advise this one—a simple and robust gun that carries the buckshot quite well. Go on. See how it feels. You will find it is quite easy to handle and excellent for your first hunt.

—All this weaponry—it is quite impressive!

—Yes. One can see that a lot of progress has been made with weapons. People always want to have something more powerful and more performing. It is a form of snobbery, I have to admit—like sports cars and golf clubs. But, you know, hunting nowadays is a sport before anything else. It has been a long time since one had to hunt to get the food they need.

—And then, all these people and all this weaponry—what is it all about?

—Well, today, we have organized a hunt for wild boars on the domain of the count. We have one every winter. Without the annual cull, the wild pigs multiply and damage the crops. Recently, they have even dug holes in two of the golf-course greens to look for roots. This is unbearable!

—That's interesting. I thought they only ate acorns in the woods.

—Usually, yes, but in winter, they become bolder and go out, and this can be dangerous for the walkers and the mushrooms hunters. Actually, for today, we have located a herd. An old male, two or three females, and at least half a dozen of piglets—we shall get rid of these. The beaters know their position and will push them toward the shooting posts that are allocated to the hunters.

—Ah, so it is! You shoot them like that. They are herded right in front of the guns. They don't have any chance, really!

—No! The boar will probably try to lure the dogs away from the rest of the herd, and the sows will sacrifice themselves for their small ones. But normally, no one should escape. We shall have a nice table of hunting.

—A NICE one, really, indeed!

—Well, we shall be leaving soon to go to our posts. One can hear the horns of the beaters closing in. As you are a beginner, I shall pair you with Monsieur Chalais. Monsieur Chalais is one of our most prominent hunters. He has been hunting all over the world—the lion in Africa, the bear in Siberia, etc. If you could see his lounge full of trophies, you would realize it is truly exceptional!

—Thank you, but I . . . it will not be necessary!

—What is wrong with you, Monsieur? You look bizarre. Are you feeling OK? Don't mind it. It is quite common for the first time because of the excitement, the stress, and the danger. Have a drink to settle yourself, and it will pass.

—No, no, I am fine. But . . . for today, I am going to change my mind.

—Why?

—Well, you see, over the years, I have been practicing a lot of sports, but I have never experienced one where you play thirty against one to destroy an opponent who doesn't have the smallest chance.

—So, Monsieur, you are leaving?

—Yes. I believe I should better take up fishing. Please excuse me. Goodbye . . . and good slaughter!

46

Wise Ass and Yellow Jersey!

—Hey, Boss, can you hear me? Have you got your earpiece in? Who is this guy? Bib Number 135?

—Wait, I'll check. Bib Number 135 . . . it's a wop—Fabrizzio Lecampi. Never heard of him. He belongs to the team Dolce Vita. Certainly a gregario (*1). He has never won anything.

—Then why did he come to get me, this idiot? I was cushy in my solitary breakaway, and I was scoring plenty of points for our team—polka-dot jersey, intermediary sprints, and combativity.

—Well, it will be one of these guys who want to be noticed. A stage victory is the dream of this sort of bicycle racer. One cannot blame him. For now, if he wants to win his stage, he will have to go for it, and you can benefit from this opportunity. You can use him as a locomotive.

—Do you really think so, Boss? I am at 2'22" at the general. When the others see that, they will react, and we will get caught in no time.

—It is not sure. You will have to play it smart. Don't forget that the finish is a false flat, and there, it will be every man for himself. Leave the wop to roll like a logger in the plain, and at the beginning of the climb, pretend you are relaying but keep your gas under the pedal. Just be sure to maintain the gap as long as possible. Try to look tired. Then at the two-kilometer mark, *paf*! You slip out from under his nose, and he will not see you again. If this works, you will not only win the stage but also have a good chance of picking up the jersey!

—Yes, I understand, Boss, but nonetheless, I don't trust these wops. Look at him. He is talking with his team director. In my opinion, they are cooking something up. By the way, how far are we now from the finish line? Ah! Seven kilometers? Of which three are for the last climb. It is still quite a long way. And the peloton, how far behind is it? 1'32"? Of course, it is a bit tight. But with the two of us, we can do it if he runs fully, this dummy.

—You could try to talk to him to see what he has in mind?

—OK, I shall try. But what am I going to say?

—Negotiate! Tell him that if he sets the pace for you and if you take the jersey, you will give him the stage's prize money even if you win it. And if he is still with you two hundred meters from the line, you will just pretend to sprint to let him cross first.

—This sounds like a good plan. I will talk to him now.

—OK, do so and come back to my car so that we can set our strategy.

—Now then, what did he say?

—That guy, he is crazy! Boss, can you believe it? He suggested exactly the same thing. He said that if I ran for him and that I don't push too hard in the sprint, he will give me the stage's prize money. He wants to have his name in the papers!

—Hell, he is nuts, that guy!

—I told you, Boss. With these wops, you have to take care. They know all the tricks. So what are we doing now?

—Shut up and pedal! Let me think.

—Hey, Boss! BOSS! While we were talking and you were thinking, he attacked. Look over there. He's gone!

—The little asshole!

—I told you, Boss. Wops—

—Yes, I know! I KNOW!

*1. *Gregario*—a term initially used by Italian cycling teams to name a team member who was just there to do all the chores (carry drinks, give wheels, set the pace, etc.) and sacrifice themselves unconditionally for the team leader.

47

Parity, Parity, Parity!

—Monsieur Department Chief, we have received a reminder about the recommendations of the ministry concerning the enforcement of the parity requirements in our service.

—What parity are you talking about?

—The parity between men and women, of course. There are still no laws concerning the other possible parities, but we had better prepare for them. They will come.

—So what are they blaming us for?

—Well, if we count our staff, we have two telephonists, three typists, two cleaners, one receptionist, one person in charge of the mail, three administrative officers, and one computer technician.

—And what is the problem? They have been here for years, and the service is functioning very well.

—Yes, but it happens that most of them are females—all but two.

—So what? If they are competent, who does that upset?

—Well, it is about the statistics of the ministry and of the government—

—I don't give a damn about the ministry's statistics. I wish they had something better to do and were much more productive!

—Alas, they are pushing these reforms, and as a result, they are asking us to move some staff. They want us to make some exchanges with other departments that have a disproportionate number of male staff.

—But this is idiotic. These chumps are going to screw up an efficient team for the sake of silly statistics and principles! I refuse!

—I am afraid that it is not possible to decline. What is more, starting now, you will have to apply a positive discrimination to all future recruitment until the gender balance is reached.

—But this is delirious. It is the political correctness of "between the legs," not of parity!

—We are led to believe that some people think this is quite important. But now, what are we going to do, Monsieur Department Chief?

—Well, please take note. I am going to dictate to you a little confidential note that is to be sent to the deputy minister who is overseeing us. Are you ready? Let's go:

Monsieur Minister

Regarding your note concerning the implementation of the law of parity, I have the pleasure of informing you that I am proceeding positively on the matter to reform my department. All our staff members will be required to undergo tests that will determine their genders. In case of a disagreement over a result, a supplementary examination will be proposed.

Following this, the staff members who will express the wish to change sex will be given an appropriate delay to undertake the necessary treatment. This could take several years with the current techniques. Keeping in mind that these staff members have permanent appointments at their posts, one will have to wait for the results of these procedures before including these posts in the staff-transfer lists.

A staff member who wishes to only change department will then have to wait for the result of the above-mentioned procedure before completing their mutation request. We must also consider the needs of the service and the progress of our parity rate. These employees will have to be given sufficient time to make their decisions. The duration of this will have to be negotiated with the unions.

It goes without saying that these changes will take time to implement as well as considerable expense. A rough estimation of the costs involved (medical costs, leaves, transfers, removal expenses, furniture, and possible court costs) could amount to 15,000 euros per employee involved. For our department alone, this may easily result in an increase of expenses of over

150,000 euros. As yet, this sum has not been allocated to our budget and can only be included in the next financial year.

During this period of strict budget restrictions, I cannot see how I can manage to face these extra expenses with my existing budget.

Therefore, in consideration of all the above and while waiting for more complete instructions and guidelines and until the necessary funds are added to my department's budget, I regret to inform you that I have to suspend sine die (*2) the parity requirements referred to in your letter.

—You are really going to send this to the minister?

—The heck I will! I actually know him quite well. I am sure that he will be quite happy to have some excuses to procrastinate. You know, these "between the legs" stories, gender and parity, etc.—all of this is bullshit meant to satisfy some activists, but in reality, we are governed with what is in the pockets of the state, not in the underwear of the public servants. Ah! You will see that for many of these nice people, it is easier to open their mouths than open their purses, and I'm not even talking about opening their zippers!

—But, nevertheless, you are laying it on heavy!

—Don't worry. The number 1 rule of the administration is to curl down one's back and wait for the next change of minister. One can always claim parity, parity, parity, but when you have no money, the good thing to do is to do nothing! Everything else is only political posturing!

*1. *Parity*: In some countries, *parity* refers to equal opportunities for employment and promotion in consideration of race, sex, etc.

*2. *Sine die*—a legal term that means that the case action is stopped without indication of when it might continue.

48

Allez Les Bleus! (*1)

—Allez les bleus! Allez les bleus! Allez!

—How much is left to play?

—Ten minutes, maybe, plus extra time.

—Then, for God's sake, why are they waiting to score a goal? We are world champions, aren't we?

—Yes, we are, but the other team do not seem to have been told that. They don't want to let us win, it seems!

—Wait! You will see! All of this is part of their tactics. You let the others get tired, and *bang*, you change rhythm and take them unawares, and then they are outflanked.

—That would be about time now! Allez les bleus! Allez!

—But what the hell are they doing? They have lost the ball again. Watch for the counterattack! Damn! This winger is hell on wheels! He made a fool of Babalam again! Watch out! He is going to cut back! NO!

—Here we are! Goal! What else would you expect with such a defense! And now, how much time left?

—Well, about seven minutes, I believe.

—Allez les bleus! Allez les bleus! It is not finished!

—Oh dear! Go forward instead of passing between our fullbacks! It's not the moment for making careful calculations! Allez! Kick forward!

—But no! Good God! Not this! This cannot be true. When you cannot even dribble, you should pass! Argh, one more lost ball!

—Get the bloody idiot off the pitch! Why is the coach waiting and not replacing him?

—The coach? Look at him! He doesn't know what to do! This one, I have no idea where they found him. If it was my call, he would be packing his bag before long!

—Ah! Now we are playing. Touch for us. Allez les bleus! Allez!

—Good. Now change of wing. Very good, but he is alone! Where the hell is the offensive support? And there it is—we have lost the ball again!

—The others are playing the counter. Watch out! They are fast! My gosh, stand up and fight, you bastards! Attack the guy in possession! No! Not like that! The idiot! Free kick and yellow card. This free kick is in a good position for them. Come on, guys! Make the wall, quick! How much time now? Dear, we are already in extra time. Come on! They must not score now and after! Everybody has to go forward for a counterattack and the equalizer! We can still save this! Allez les bleus! Allez les bleus! Allez! AH! NO!

—Did you see that? Right into the top corner! What a goal!

—Yeah! The keeper could do nothing. When it doesn't want to go our way, it won't. Two to zero—the carrots are cooked now!

—That's it! The referee has blown his whistle! Game over. Come on, guys. We have seen enough. let's get outta there!

—Hey, mates! Did you see the players parking over there with all the flashy cars?

—Yeah! It is like a sports cars showroom: Porsche, Aston Martin, Ferrari—there is even a Lambo! You don't see many of them around. Here, guys! These are poor people cars, or I know nothing about it!

—And did you see the blonde waiting near the BMW over there? Another luxury body, no?

—The warrior's rest! Aha!

—See there? The players are coming out of the changing rooms. Apparently, they don't really look too worried about losing the game!

—Hey, guys, this could be a good time to get autographs. There are not too many people waiting. Let's call out to the players. "Hey, hey, les bleus! Allez les bleus! We are with you!" They cannot hear me. Come on, you guys! The rest of you, let's all call out—

—Shut your fucking mouth! Allez the blues? Yes, go to hell with your flashy wheelboxes and your upscale tarts. Myself, at the moment, when you call blue, I see red!

*1. "Allez les bleus! [Come on the blues!]"—usual French-team supporter's slogan

49

Everyone has Their Cross to Bear!

—Good morning, Madame. I would like to file a claim for the Légion d'honneur (*1).

—Ah! You don't have it already?

—No. Probably an oversight.

—You want to apply in a civilian capacity, I suppose.

—Yes. What do I need to produce for my claim?

—Your civil-status data, of course, but you will also have to give the reasons of your claim and why you deserve to be distinguished. You will also have to produce the patronage of some notables citizens who are recommending you for this national distinction.

—Ah, good, and what is working better at the moment?

—Well, it depends. There is the political aspect. Are you an elected official? Local or regional? If yes, which party do you represent and for how long? Without this, you will need the support of at least one MP.

—And if I don't have that?

—Then it will be more difficult. You will have to provide proof of exceptional services that were achieved for the benefit of society.

—What sort of services, for example?

—Well, a bit of everything: your membership at a diverse association, especially ecologic or sporting, or a service in the artistic and cultural domains; your administrative career; your local notoriety; etc. The more the better.

—Well, hmm. I see, but me, I am rather a discreet person.

—Then, why do you want to obtain this distinction?

—Ah, to be like everybody else!

—You might want that, but you will still have to fill out a claim. In fact, you are not supposed to do that yourself. Someone else is supposed to do it for you. You will also need to have fifty supporting signatures. In addition, you will have to pay the taxes and also buy your medal.

—Ah, I did not know that. And how much does that all cost approximately?

—Well, you may have to expect about a thousand euros! But this still does not include the cost for the traditional wine reception.

—Hmm . . . can this not be refunded by some sort of social fund? What happens if you cannot afford it? You cannot receive the distinction?

—No, unfortunately not, I am afraid.

—Damn, I did not see this coming! But please, tell me, Madame.

—Yes?

—By any chance, you would not have a secondhand one available for sale?

*1. Légion d'honneur, created by Napoléon, is France's highest distinction.

50

Elections, Booby Trap!

—Ah, my dear, thank you for coming. I need your advice.

—I am here to help, as you know, Monsieur President.

—Yes, you are my political advisor, and this is the moment to show it.

—Go on! What is the problem this time?

—Yes, you know the situation with the upcoming election. At the moment, the polls show that we are stagnating at 18 percent. We must do something!

—Certainly, we need to find 4 or 5 percent more votes to make it safe, I know. Have you already approached all the possible alliances?

—Yes, I tried to rake wide, but that was not sufficient.

—Now what?

—Well, there is still this Lemarchand with his small centrist party. He is precisely weighting 4 or 5 percent, but he did not bother to hear about an alliance. He wants to play it personal! All of this to win one or two seats!

—What an idiot!

—Yes, an idiot. But nevertheless, how to pick up his votes?

—Simply put, we need to destabilize him and force him to negotiate.

—Exactly!

—And we shall use the usual methods, I suppose? It always revolves around the same three things: money, sex, and family!

—Yes. I suppose that you already have information on him in your little papers. Let's see: Money?

—Money, in his case, is rather transparent. We have been combing through his tax declarations. No discreet bank account in Switzerland or Bermuda. No shell companies. No suspicious financial manipulations. No sudden personal gain. We have investigated everything. This guy is as clean as a whistle.

—That is not possible. Something like that still exists? I was thinking that, since de Gaulle, these "clean as a whistle" specimens had disappeared!

—You will have to change your mind. It seems there are still some idealists in politics, and they are a danger!

—Well then, let's move to the sex chapter. He is young and good-looking. He must have had some opportunities, no?

—Without a doubt. But his marriage seems to be holding in spite of the political life. There is nothing that we know of. No suspicious relationship, no chambermaid affair, no hidden second life, and no special tastes.

—And his wife? What is she doing when he is attending the parliamentary sessions all night? She is just watching TV at home?

—You have to believe so. We found nothing we can use.

—Shit! A paragon of virtue! Of all people, we had to get a guy like that. This is just our luck!

—Yes, and it doesn't get any better for us. On the family chapter, we found a big fat zero. No fictive jobs, no hidden benefits for his parents, and no abuses of position—nothing we could make a fuss about in the media.

—We are in trouble. But nevertheless, we have to catch him with something. So do you have any suggestions? This is what you are paid for!

—We shall have to set up some mischief—just for the period of the elections—even if we might need to deny any knowledge of these actions afterward or let the things settle down and be forgotten to prevent any possible fallout.

—OK, give me the details.

—Well, we need to release several stories at around the same time. Even though they will be bogus, the whole picture will seem plausible, and his public image and reputation will really suffer.

—Practically, how will this work?

—Practically, we shall be attacking on all the fronts simultaneously. Money first. We shall muddle through to get him to be invited to become the patron of some charitable society. He won't be able to refuse. But, bad luck, we will also have arranged some under-the-table misappropriations and fiddling of the books, such as cash disappearing, allowances finding welcoming pockets, etc. Scandal is guaranteed! Of course, he will not be directly involved, but he will still be hit by the splatters.

—Very good. This is easy. There are plenty of societies like that. And then what?

—Then sex! We'll find a pretty little thing who is not shy that we are going to put within reach of his paws. Even if the thing is not successful and he manages to resist her charms, we will make sure that she is beside him for a few snapshots when they are at some cocktail party or reception. There are paparazzi and ass-wiping people magazines who specialize in this sort of grubby stuff. You just need to raise a hint of suspicion without having any evidence or proof. People love this sort of thing.

—Good! Do you have something more? Family?

—Yes! But political family. There is nothing worse than internal quarrels in political families. You know a lot about this, yourself, of course!

—Sure I do. But what do you have in mind?

—Ah, well, there is always a little smart-ass who is ambitious and would like to replace the caliph. You only need to find this little wise guy and have a chat with him, and I already have a possible candidate in mind.

—And the little smart-ass, how will he operate?

—Easy! He will show off his face in the media at every opportunity and portray himself as a potential challenger or successor. This will create some nice internal division in the party. Of course, we shall be discreetly whispering a few things into his ear to motivate him.

—OK, I see the picture. If we agree on that, all of this must be released just one month before the elections.

—That should not be a problem if we start preparing now.

—It could also be good to have some judges in our pocket! A nice little indictment for Monsieur Lemarchand! That proved to be an effective strategy with others in the past.

—No, not this time. Don't forget, we have nothing solid on him, and that could come back to bite us in the bum if the judge smells a rat.

—Good! One last thing: My name must not be linked in any way to any of these actions. He will probably try to find out where the blows are coming from, and he might even guess right.

—I know my job! On the contrary, I suggest that you butter him up at every opportunity. Act as if you were his best friend, and pretend you are convinced by his ideas and ready to make concessions.

—That, I am good at! Don't be afraid. I am no greenhorn in politics!

—So do we go for it?

—We will. It's up to you to show what you can do!

—Don't worry. In three weeks, you will see—this guy will come to you and be eating from your hand!

—I am counting on that!

—Then, goodbye, Monsieur President. I will keep you informed.

—Yes, but, please, wait—there is still one more thing we must talk about before you leave.

—Yes?

—Well, I would just like to be sure that you have not recorded this conversation without me knowing. I have here a little electronic detecting gadget, which is quite practical for this sort of thing!

—But, Monsieur President, you know me!

—Precisely—I know you too well! And between people belonging to the same world, it is better to be safe than sorry, isn't it?

51

All Together, Comrades!

—Could I have a word with you, Comrade Delegate?

—Certainly, Comrade. What is the matter?

—Well, um, I did not understand too well some points in your speech. I want to ask you a few questions before we leave for the demonstration.

—Ah! And which ones?

—You shouted, "Down with the capitalism! Down with the bosses! Down with the infernal production rates! Down with the people starvers! Down with the profiteers and exploiters!"

—Yes, this is what we shout during such circumstances. It is important to lift the spirits of the troops before a day of action.

—Yes, I understand that capitalism is the exploitation of man by man and we are the exploited!

—You have understood perfectly, Comrade, so what is bothering you?

—Ah, but we—if we are against the capitalism, the capitalists, the bosses, the banks, and all of that, what do we actually stand for?

—It's obvious! We stand for the opposite of all those things. We share instead of grab at the expense of others. Communism is the reverse of the capitalism!

—Ah, well, but then who will work for us? The bosses, the bankers, and the politicians? If nobody is working, what will we have to share?

—Comrade, I believe that you ask yourself too many questions. We are not that far along with our struggle at the moment. We are in the protesting-and-claiming stage, not in the restructuring phase. Everything has its own time. First, we have to break the system, and then we will see.

—And at the moment, we are breaking shop windows and bus shelters, no?

—Come on, Comrade! The people's anger may lead to some little excesses, but these can be excused when the cause is right. Anyways, they provide some work to those who are tasked with repairing the damages. You must not think that the struggle of the classes will progress if we remain soft and gentle. The struggle of the classes! You have heard about it, I hope, Comrade. It is our hardest fight!

—The struggle of the classes? Yes, um . . . yes, I remember now. When I was about ten years old and at school, the older boys of the other classes were bullying and racketing us. We had to take care and stay out of trouble! And then later, when I was doing my military-service basic training with our age class, the sergeant was always yelling at us to make us march properly.

—So you see, Comrade, the struggle of the classes is everywhere in your life, and now you have to march again. But this time, it is against the empowered who are oppressing us and the bosses who are exploiting us.

—I have understood, Comrade Delegate, but me, I don't have a boss. So who should I shout against?

—How is that possible? You don't have a boss?

—Yes, I do not. I am jobless.

—There! You see? You are a victim of the system, and it is precisely for you that we are fighting! Come on, Comrade! Let's go! You will be in the first row for the final fight! Goodbye! Have a good demonstration! We are counting on you!

—Goodbye, Comrade Delegate!

—As for me, it may not be all the same, but I would rather have a job and a boss instead of brandishing this stupid banner!

52

Little Profits!

—Monsieur Prefect?

—Yes, what is it, Monsieur Administrative Director?

—It's about today's farmer demonstration. They have started gathering in front of the prefecture's gates.

—Good! We can always rely on these ones to be punctual. Have you taken all the precautions? Are the gates properly closed?

—Yes, everything is locked up, and the CRS (*1) are stationed at the front to prevent demonstrators from climbing the gates. During the last demonstration, they had been torn away, and the cement used in the repairs has barely dried!

—Great. Have the shutters been closed on all the windows? Have all the objects that could be used as projectiles been taken away?

—Everything is ready, Monsieur Prefect. And we are in direct contact with the commanding officer of the gendarmerie, the firemen, the SAMU (*2), and the municipality services. And the accesses of the nearby streets are all controlled.

—This is perfect. How many of them are there?

—I would say around three hundred, but there are still some more coming.

—And what do they want?

—Ha! Always the usual things: better agricultural prices for the producers, increased allocations, and more benefits in the retirement system.

—Oh, we cannot do much for them at our regional level. These are national issues, and some may even be international ones.

—Yes, and that is why they are demonstrating everywhere in the country at the same time.

—A lot of good, they are doing! Alas, I am afraid that many of these poor wretches are condemned. We can only postpone the inevitable.

—Yes, Monsieur Prefect, but in the meantime, they are in the streets, and we have to manage the situation without getting into trouble. The ministry instructions are "Lay low' and "Drag things out."

—I suppose they did not come with nothing?

—What do you mean "with nothing"?

—Well, usually, they bring trailers full of different vegetables or fruits that they drop down in front of the main door. Last time, there were artichokes and peaches. Even after we got rid of those that were crushed, there was enough for the prefecture's staff to enjoy for a week!

—Can you see if they have something? It would be great if this time, they had rock melons or potatoes. It is the new season now. And those products will be fresh and taste much better than those in the supermarkets!

—I see a trailer and some guys with shovels. Oh dear—this time, it is serious. I think that they are going to spill some manure! Ah, they have also started to set bales of straw and packaging on fire!

—This is classic and belongs to their usual scenario. Tell the police forces to stay calm and only call a fire truck if it looks like the fire will spread. Well, I suppose that they will want me to receive a delegation and a list of claims. Can you send one of our staff as an emissary so they can arrange what is needed? That will speed things up, and when they are tired of shouting, they will be able to finish and go home earlier. Ah, the internal phone! Please take the call. Who is it?

—Monsieur Prefect, it's Madame, your wife. She wants to remind you not to let them in with their boots covered with mud and manure. Last time, it was necessary to clean all the carpets and deodorize the lounge. "Can you receive them at the doorway?" she said.

—Wait! Put her through. Thank you! Allo, Françoise? Yes, I understand that for the carpets—no, I shall not invite them into the main lounge. No, I expect that I will go out to meet them myself. No, I am not crazy. Am I going to be bombarded with rotten eggs and tomatoes like at the last ministerial visit? No, I don't think so. They seem quite calm today. You're tired of having my uniforms cleaned up? Ah, you don't have a replacement left? That changes everything. I shall receive them in the public reception room. It has a tiled floor. Yes, it is safer there. OK, see you later! Bye!

—So, Monsieur Prefect, I think I have understood that—

—That women always get their way in the end, as you can see. One could ask oneself who is really governing this country! Now then, quickly give orders to prepare a room with a tiled floor that is easy to clean and set up there a dozen chairs around a large wooden table. They will feel at home—like at the farm! Well, how are things outside?

—They released a few piglets! The CRS are trying to catch them. Everybody is laughing!

—Good, it seems they are having some fun and the situation is unlikely to deteriorate. At least, that's something!

—Ah! Here they come! A delegation is approaching the main gate.

—That's good. Please, let them come in—but no more than eight or so. That will be plenty. I will receive them with you. Yes, you can let the press come in for a picture.

—Phew! It's done, Monsieur Prefect! They are outside now, and their leader is talking with the megaphone, explaining to his troops what happened at the meeting. There's a bit of grunting, it seems!

—Yes, but what were they expecting? I could not do better than promise to take their complaints to Paris and tell them that as far as I was concerned, I understood their concerns as I, myself, am the grandson of a peasant, and I will be fully supporting them to the best of my ability.

—Yes, but you talked about suppressing the regional tax on the local markets, That may have been going a little too far, no?

—Not at all. Anyways, it will indeed be suppressed—even if it is likely that it will be replaced later by another tax! So why not benefit from a positive announcement that we can make today?

—Well, it calmed them down, and they think they have gained something. Ah, they are starting to disperse. So this time, everything went well. You played it smart!

—Yes! Please call the minister for me. I wish to give him an oral report.

—Allo? The minister's office? Yes, it is the prefecture of—good. Please hold. I will put him on. Monsieur Prefect, Monsieur Minister would like to talk to you personally. Here he is!

—Allo, Jean Pierre? No, no problem. Everything went fine. No, no damages. What? Potatoes? No, this time, they have only dumped manure. Yes, too bad. It's a pity that we cannot ask them for something better, eh? Yes, they were excellent, and so were the artichokes. Yes, we will just have to wait for the next demonstration, and I will certainly keep a box or two for you. Yes, I promise. Please, pass on my regards to Madame. Thank you and goodbye!

—And now, Monsieur Prefect, concerning the cleaning?

—OK. See to that with our municipal services. Ah, the internal phone again! Take the call, please. Thank you!

—Monsieur Prefect, it is Madame Prefect again.

—Yes, and what does she want this time? Everything happened just as she wanted, no?

—She asked that when the pile of manure is cleaned up, could we please keep a few bags to put in your private vegetable garden and on the flower beds of the prefecture. She said that's better than wasting it by throwing it away at the dump. True bio manure—it's worth a fortune in the garden centers!

—That's OK with me. Please do the necessary—by the way, I wonder if we should not also keep a few bags for the minister's wife!

*1. The Compagnies Républicaines de Sécurité (CRS) are the reserve of the French National Police and are primarily involved in general security duties.

*2. The Service d'Aide Médicale Urgente (SAMU) provides ambulances and other emergency medical services.

53

Memories from beyond the Grave

—Good day, Monsieur. Are you the administrator of this municipal cemetery?

—In some ways, yes. What can I do for you?

—I would like to buy a burial plot.

—Ah! You have had a fatality in your family. My condolences, Monsieur.

—No, it is for me.

—For you? You seem to be in pretty good health.

—Yes, I am fine. But I would like to have things prepared in advance. If something happens to me, I would not want to be caught flat-footed.

—I understand your concern. Effectively, you can reserve a plot in advance, but you will have to pay a yearly fee even if you are not using it now.

—No problem. That seems fair so long as the price is reasonable.

—Would the plot be for you alone or for several persons? In the latter case, it would be cheaper as you could share the cost.

—No, that is out of the question. I like to be quiet at home. No co-owned rental—not now and not ever.

—Will you have a grave, a funeral stone, or simply a cross?

—Hmm . . . I have not yet made up my mind about this. What are the advantages to consider?

—Well, it often depends on the family members. Quite often they want a tombstone. First, because it is easier to maintain, and then because they want to make sure that with two hundred kilograms on the belly, the deceased will not have the fantasy of getting out and meddling with what is no longer his business.

—Don't worry. Me, I am quite quiet, and when I am comfortable somewhere, I stay!

—Would you like to come with me and choose a place now? In fact, it is an old cemetery, and all the best places had been taken already for a long time, but we have recently bought some more land for an extension, and there are good opportunities at the moment.

—Sure, let's do it. I will follow you. Have you been working here long?

—Yes! Over twenty years, and I know everybody in here. Here we are. These are the most recent graves. Some are still quite fresh.

—I see, but I also hear. It is quite bizarre—like there's music coming out of a grave!

—That's true. You know, sometimes people have unusual whims—as if they, in some way, would like to still be connected to life. This one wanted to be buried with his Walkman and his favorite music recordings. His family placed stereo loudspeakers in his coffin plus a battery power source to keep them playing. So far, they have been working quite well, but the batteries will die at some point, and that will be the the end of it.

—They could not just have popped headphones on the deceased instead of using these loudspeakers? This could be disturbing the neighbors—even if the music is muffled by the earth.

—You know, the neighbors are not really likely to complain.

—Yes, of course—I had forgotten. You have other interesting cases like this one?

—Yes, and they happen more often than you would expect. The most common thing is for people to leave a mobile phone in the coffin. You never know, they say. From time to time, they even call the number. They say that they feel a bit weird when they hear the voice of the deceased on the voice mail. For me, I also feel strange when I hear a phone ringing as I move around the cemetery. I am always afraid that somebody will pick up the phone and answer it!

—Ah! Yes, that would be a good gag for a horror movie!

—If you say so. And then there are also those who want to depart this life with their familiar objects or food. See down there, the 247b—he wanted to be buried with six bottles of Saint Emilion Grand Cru, and guess what? The next day, we had to reopen the grave because his family found out that they had forgotten to leave a corkscrew! Ah, we have arrived. Here—this could be a good spot.

—Yes, it looks quiet and is in a lovely position.

—And there are good neighbors. This one was a former gendarmerie officer, and on the other side, it is also a policeman. Quite a coincidence!

—Yes, but I don't feel too comfortable with the idea of spending my death between two policemen. It may look wrong, no?

—As you wish. Here is another free plot. Nearby, there are good people that I knew quite well. The husband had retired from the railways, and unfortunately, his wife succumbed to meningitis.

—Oh dear! But that is very contagious! I don't know if—

—But, really, in your situation, when you will move in, you will not be at risk anymore!

—Yes, that is true, but nevertheless—what about there—that empty lawn?

—That will be the extension, but I would not recommend it at this stage.

—Why?

—Because the kids from the nearby housing complex, they go there to play soccer, and they often use the crosses as goalposts. I try to chase them out, but they always come back because they have nowhere else to go other than the road. So I often look the other way just as long as they are not breaking anything.

—Ah, and over there, the three people with the shovels—they must be your gravediggers. Are you expecting a new resident today?

—No, there are no burials scheduled, but I can guess why they are here.

—Ah, and why?

—Well, they are beside the 304a, where someone had been buried yesterday. It happens that, that guy was an absolute sports fanatic, and at the time of his death, he was really frustrated that he would miss the next France versus England rugby match—so much that on his deathbed, he made the family promise that they would leave a small, battery-powered TV in his grave that was all set to turn on and transmit just before the kickoff.

—Wow! It is incredible how people can be so naive and sometimes want to ignore the reality of death. But your gravediggers—what are they doing there while leaning on their shovels? They don't seem to be doing much work!

—But what do you think? They are watching the match! They will fill the grave after!

54

In Vino Veritas! (*1)

—Monseigneur, you summoned me, and I came immediately. What is going on?

—Yes, Reverend. There is a very serious case concerning you.

—I don't understand. Can you enlighten me?

—We have received an allegation about your behavior concerning a sexual assault of one of the children attending the catechism in your parish. We have a letter from the parents of a certain Gilles Dubois. Is he one of your parishioners?

—Yes, and what do they say?

—Their child came back from the catechism and complained that while he was saying his prayers after having been heard in confession, you took his pants off and then spanked him in front of the altar. Do you admit the facts?

—Ah, the little bastard!

—Pardon, Reverend? How dare you talk like that!

—Excuse me, Monseigneur, but I couldn't help myself. This Gilles Dubois is a real scoundrel. He seems to be possessed by the need to do mischief. He is diabolic and perverse.

—That may be true, but it does not justify such a treatment. By the way, what did he do to make you forget your duties as a man of the church and of peace?

—Well, Monseigneur, for several days, I had noticed that my communion wine had a horrible taste. It was absolutely undrinkable—or at least the wine I put in a flask on the altar when I am preparing for my daily mass. The wine that was still in the bottle, which I keep locked up in the sacristy, still tasted fine. I started to think that somebody was tampering with the communion wine on the altar because the level did not get lower.

—Yes, and what did you do?

—So I purchased one of those tiny security cameras that exist now, and I placed it somewhere discreet so it could cover the altar. Such a device has a sensor, and it starts recording automatically after it detects the faintest motion inside their range of view. They give excellent picture quality even when they are inside the clair-obscure of a church.

—And the result of this monitoring is?

—Gilles Dubois was filmed drinking surreptitiously a few sips from the flask on the altar.

—That is quite common. Many choir boys have done that over the years.

—Yes, but usually, they just add a bit of water to mask their crime. But not Gilles Dubois. He simply opened his zipper and replenished the container with his own natural product!

—Ah, the little bastard! That is absolutely disgusting!

—You see, Monseigneur? Now you are calling him that yourself!

—Then what did you do? The boy's revolting behavior can explain your anger but not the actions that you are accused of.

—Well, I wanted to catch him red-handed, so the next time I planned to record him, I hid myself in a confessional and waited for the end of the catechism. I did not have to wait very long. After the catechism was finished and everyone went out, I saw this Gilles Dubois come back inside under the pretext of wanting to say a prayer at the altar, and he perpetrated his crime again! Then, at the moment where he had dropped his pants to replace the pilfered wine, I sprang out of my hiding place and caught him, put him over my knee just as he was, and administered the spanking that he fully deserved!

—That, he indeed deserved, for sure, but your anger does not excuse your action. Those days are gone. But in the parents' letter, there is mention of a witness, a so-called Mademoiselle Prudence Piqueboeuf, who was the involuntary spectator of this scene.

—Ah, that one! A church mouse if ever there was one!

—Monsieur Reverend, you are talking about one of your parishioners! I ask you to be more respectful. Unfortunately, her testimony is shattering. She says she saw your hand over the naked anatomy of young Dubois and that the kid bent over your knees was weeping.

—Effectively, but she is a simpleminded soul who is always hanging around in the church. She must have been attracted by the shouting. She came, saw the scene, raised her hands to heaven, and ran away while shouting, "The devil! The devil!" The appearances are against me.

—That's the least you can say! And after that, what did you do with the kid?

—I let him go and told him not to do it again. Otherwise, he would be expelled from the catechism, but he looked at me with an evil eye and shouted back, "Bloody vicar of my balls, I am going to get revenge, and I know how to do it!"

—Yes, he certainly did, and now he is getting it because it is your word against that of two others. And you know what a churchman's parole is worth nowadays—with all the dirty news published in the press. Even if you are innocent—and I believe you are—you will be lynched by the media, and there will be nothing we can do about it. All the superiors in the hierarchy will simply open their umbrellas, and you will be removed from your parish and sent for repentance to some lost monastery.

—So what can we do now?

—Nothing, I'm afraid. We could try to explain the truth to the boy's parents and to this Prudence Piqueboeuf, but we only have proof that the kid was drinking the wine—nothing on the facts that you are accused of and the scene that followed.

—Ah, but wait, Monseigneur! I have just thought of something!

—That would be about time, and what is it?

—Well, I just realized that I forgot to turn off the camera and remove it. So it is probable that it was still working and recorded the whole scene!

—If this is true, you are saved! I believe that we will see that the hand of God was protecting you when your own hands were busy with the bottom of that scoundrel!

—Yes, but has our Lord himself not been subjected to righteous angers?

—Let's not get into that now. More importantly, send me this video by mail, and I shall show it to the Dubois family and to Mademoiselle Piqueboeuf. They will not be able to maintain their claim and argue for the innocence of the lad. I believe that this Gilles Dubois will have a rough time if his father's hand is as fast as yours. I will take care of this affair while you quietly go back to your parish. Au revoir. Off you go.

—Thank you, Monseigneur!

—But wait! Tell me, what do you use for your mass wine?

—A quite-sympathetic little burgundy, which is generously given to me by one of my parishioners who happens to be a winemaker. You know, our village is inside a classified AOC area (*2).

—If it is as good as you say, I would like to try some. Could you get me a few bottles?

—My pleasure, Monseigneur. You will not be disappointed, you will see.

—I hope so because my own mass wine has been tasting a little strange recently. I don't know—it can be just an impression. Anyways, thank you in advance.

—It is as good as done, Monseigneur.

—Ah, yes, and one more thing—while you are at it, could you also lend me this spying device you were talking about? One never knows!

*1. "In vino veritas"—a Latin saying that means "In wine lies the truth."
*2. *AOC* is used to describe wines that come from a specific area in France.

55

Emergency!

—Doctor! Doctor! An emergency case has just arrived!

—OK, I am preparing myself, and I will come immediately. Meanwhile, tell me quickly about the case.

—It is a soccer player. He has been kicked in the balls!

—That happens in this game, but usually, it does not justify one being sent to the ED (*1).

—This time, yes. It was a terrible kick, and the victim is still unconscious.

—Aïe, aïe, aïe! That could be serious! Let's go. I am ready.

—Well, effectively, it is not looking pretty! Have you already done the x-rays? Yes? Good. Let's have a look. Hmm. Apparently, the left testicle has suffered a lot. In fact, it seems to have literally exploded. There is also a torsion (*2). Not good. I believe that the best we can do is limit the damage. We will not be able to repair it. It is better to take it out completely and drain the hematoma to reduce the risk of infection. The other one seems to be in a better state, and we should be able to save it! Hopefully, that gentleman will still be able to present himself in front of the ladies with some chance of success! OK, let's go! Take him to the operating room!

—How are the vital signs? His blood pressure is in his socks? Put him under assistance so long as we are operating. OK, everybody is ready? Anesthesia is OK? Here we go.

—Look here, Doctor! He has an internal hemorrhage!

—Yes, I see it. Suck this pocket of blood so we can see where it is coming from. OK, I found it. We just need to suture. There. Good. Phew!

—He seems stable, so now, let's see the balls. Oh dear, the left one has been pulped. Poor guy. Come on, we need to remove it and clean up the mess.

—OK, it's done! Now you can stitch him up. Thank you. How is he doing? Good. The initial state of shock seems to be diminishing. He will make it, but he will not be able to piss for at least a week without jumping through the roof. Fit him with a catheter to help and, of course, do all the usual post-op treatment and support. But what is all that noise outside?

—Apparently, there is a group of club supporters at the reception area who have come to get some news. They are arguing that it was not fair that the culprit was not even yellow-carded by the referee when it should have been a red!

—These idiots are discussing the colors of cards when we are trying to save their champion?

—Alas, yes, and there are also two people at the reception area who would like to see you when you have finished.

—And who are these two people?

—I believe they are the president of the club and the head coach.

—What the hell do they want?

—They want to know if their star striker will be able to play in the final this Saturday. What should I say to them?

—Tell them to kick their asses out of here!

*1. *ED* (Emergency Department)
*2. *Torsion*: Testicular torsion occurs when a testicle rotates, twisting the spermatic cord that brings blood to the scrotum. The reduced blood flow causes sudden and often-severe pain and swelling

56

Michelin-Starred Junk Food!

—Chef Michel, we have a problem!

—And what is the problem?

—We just received a request for six people at 2100.

—They did not book a table and meals?

—No, but the boss accepted them because they are VIPs—a local politician with his little court, as far as I know.

—But what on earth am I going to cook for them? There is nothing left in the fridges other than little things, and it is too late now to buy something more serious.

—The boss, he said that you are the chef and you are the one who has to deal with the situation.

—He is funny, that one! Tell him to call this client back and cancel. I am not God! I cannot multiply the loaves and the fishes!

—Tell him yourself. I don't want to be yelled at. Here, I will put you through on the internal phone.

—Allo, Edouard? It's Michel. Are you crazy or what? We have literally been looted this weekend. I have only a few salads left—no meat and no fish. I will be cooking what for these guys? An omelette? And I am not even sure that we have enough eggs! What? It is not possible to cancel? Surely it's not like they just decided to eat out. They are not coming here by hazard? They could have booked like normal people, those idiots! But wait, I am thinking . . . yes, I may have an idea. It is risky, but in wartime, we must do as in wartime. Listen, call them back and warn them that it will be a surprise menu and they will have to take the potluck. You have some good wines, at least. Those will help. OK, leave it to me, but don't complain if it turns out to be a fiasco. What am I planning to do? No, I cannot tell you anything. This will be a surprise for you too. Perhaps it's better this way. OK, I am going to start working on it. There is no time to lose.

—Yes, Chef, they have gone. They looked very happy. Ah, here comes the boss. He looks pretty satisfied too. Apparently, everything has gone well.

—So, Edouard, you are breathing better?

—Listen, my old Michel, I don't know how you did it, but they swallowed everything without blinking an eye—even the bill!

—Knowing you, the bill must have been more salty than the food. How much?

—Bof! Two hundred euros per head—a misery! Price is a matter of standing for this kind of customer. This fortune du pot was great! Besides, this dinner looked pretty cool. Super well-presented and diversified! A success!

—Yeah, but I am not going to do this every day.

—Tell me, how did you manage to make the coquelet aux raisins (*1) or the sauté de marcassin à la mousse de marrons (*2) or even the délices des bois au coulis de fruits rouges (*3), and I have not even started talking about the remarkable salade de saison aux herbes du jardin (*4)?

—Well, you know, this is what the job is all about.

—Boss, somebody is knocking at the door and wants to come in.

—Ah, no. It's late. We are closed now. Ask him what he wants, and if it is for a meal, send him to the MacDo next door!

—No, Boss, he is coming from the MacDo, and he is bringing a bill.

—What? A bill? But who the hell has been ordering all of this? It cannot be us!

—But it is us, Richard. It was me!

—WHAT! YOU? Michel, a Michelin-starred chef, ordering MacDo junk food, but no, I must be dreaming! Or maybe I am afraid to understand that something has been going on.

—You have well understood. How did you expect me to find all the ingredients that I needed—the meat, the chicken, the fish, etc.? I bought all the products from them and worked with that. I cut them into pieces and added my special touch with the appropriate sauces and flavors. So the pieces of fried chicken turned into coquelets aux raisins and the minced meat of the hamburgers turned into sauté de marcassin.

—This cannot be true! I am speechless! We made them eat MacDo junk!

—But no, that was no longer MacDo food—or, at least, not really! You know, the art of cooking is to accommodate anything with everything. The sauces and the spices make the difference. With a little bit of artistic presentation, people will swallow nearly anything. It's a bit like modern art: It is ugly, but if you are told that it is beautiful, then you end up finding some beauty!

—Do you even realize the risk that you have taken and the scale of the scandal if it got out? Oh dear, what a story!

—Come on, Edouard! Look at the MacDo invoice. How much do you have to pay?

—Just less than a hundred euros!

—So do the math—100 euros on one side and 1,200 on the other. Even taking into account the 2 bottles of wine for 100 euros, you made a pretty good profit tonight, no?

—I must admit that you're right, but it is crazy!

—Desperate situations call for desperate measures.

—And great chefs! Bravo, Michel! But don't do this to me again, OK?

—What are you talking about? But if you want a good friend's advice, you should consider buying the MacDo next door if it ever comes up for sale. One never knows!

*1. Coquelet aux raisins (cockerel with grapes)
*2. Sauté de marcassin à la mousse de marrons (wild boar sauté with chestnut mousse)
*3. Délices des bois au coulis de fruits rouges (delicacies from the wood with red fruit coulis)
*4. Salade de saison aux herbes du jardin (seasonal salad with herbs from the garden)

57

March or Die!

—Well, Comrades, now we are going to vote!

—By a show of hands?

—Of course by a show of hands! We all know it is safer. So let's vote: Those in favor, lift your arms!

—Hey, you there, Comrade! Why are you lifting both of your arms? That's cheating!

—No, Comrade. I am voting for my mate who could not come.

—OK, we'll let it go this time, but if everybody was doing it like you, this would become like the Chamber of Deputies—only two or three penguins assisting and voting for the others. We would have nobody coming to our trade-union meetings. There are already not many people coming!

—OK now, those against, lift your arms!

—Hey, Comrade! Why do you lift your arm? Don't you see that you are the only one doing so?

—No, it's not that. I just wanted permission to go to the toilets.

—Do you believe you are still at school? OK, that's good. Go and hurry! So the strike has been decided with a unanimous vote. Now we have to decide on the actions we will take. Let me remind you that a day of strike is a day of action, not a day to twiddle your thumbs. I am now waiting for your suggestions!

—We could have a march and a sit-in with some speeches!

—No, we should lock the gate of the factory!

—Why not take the director hostage?

—We could build a roadblock on the motorway!

—Or on the TGV rail (*1)!

—Or a snail operation on the peripheral boulevard!

—Or tag the walls of the plant!

—Distribute leaflets at the market!

—This is good, Comrades. I see that you are not short of ideas and experience, but we have more or less tried all these actions, and on the whole, we have to admit that they have not been very effective. And sadly, some have stirred up the public opinion against us. We need something new that will really draw the attention of the people. Maybe something more ecological or humoristic.

—Yes, let's make people have fun instead of hassling them. The laugh will be on our side. This is a good idea, this one. Come on, Comrades! It is about time that we made ourselves heard!

—Maybe we could organize a lottery or a raffle, and with the money we make, we could buy sweets and distribute them to the children when their schools let them out?

—That's a bit Boy Scout, no? We should have something more active.

—A soccer or pétanque tournament?

—No, people would think that we are only trying to have a good time.

—Make an operation motorway have a free-toll day?

—That would not be easy, and we would have the cops on our tails. No, not this time.

—We could pick up all the paper and trash that are lying around in the neighborhood and empty the bags at the gate of the factory.

—Not bad. At least that idea has an environmental angle.

—Yeah, but it is a tedious and dirty job, always leaning down and dragging the bags. And also, with all these syringes that the junkies throw away, it is dangerous. No, we are not equipped for it, and it would be seen as an act of disloyal competition by our comrades who earn their living by cleaning up the town.

—And if we organized a costume parade with fancy dresses?

—Nobody would take us seriously. It's a strike, not Shrove Tuesday (*2)!

—I've got an idea! We should march nude!

—WHAT! What's the matter with you? Naked, and what else?

—Actually, me, I agree. We will certainly draw the attention of the public, the media, and even the international press.

—That is true. Look at these calendars with the rugby or soccer teams posing nude. Even old ladies have done that for a charity. It is popular and sells well.

—But if it is cold or raining, we shall catch our death from cold!

—March or die, ah-ah! If you want a result, you have to take some risks and put your life at stake!

—Hey! Have you considered our female comrades? They would possibly not agree.

—They could drape themselves with the banners or hide the strategic places with the signs.

—At least, this time, people will look at the signs!

—We could allow the use of swimsuits for those who are a bit shy.

—Why not burkinis while you are at it?

—Come on, Comrades! Don't deviate from the subject! We are laics— don't forget it!

—Laics and naked, ha ha!

—By the way, did you know that it was the Canuts (*3) of Lyon who were at the origin of the first strike and their song was "Nous sommes les canuts, nous sommes tout nus [*4]!"

—What was that? The culs nus (*5)?

—No, not culs nus. Canuts. They were the workers in the silk-weaving factories. They made terrible strikes, and a lot of them were killed by the police. It would be a tribute to them. In fact, we are their heirs, and we will continue their fight.

—For once, *we* are inheriting something! I am in favor!

—Well then, the proposal is for a nude march with maybe some in swimsuits. Shall we vote?

—Yes, let's vote!

—By a show of hands?

—No, by a show of arse! Ha ha!

*1. TGV is the name of a French high-speed rail service.

*2. Shrove Tuesday (*Mardi gras*)—children used to disguise themselves and knock on doors to get sweets and crepes.

*3. *Canuts*—very poorly paid workers who used silk-weaving machines in Lyon during the nineteenth century.

*4. "We are the Canuts, we are all nude!"

*5. Intentional confusion between *Canuts* and *culs nus* (naked asses), which sound nearly the same.

58

Miaaaaow!

Dedicated to my cat, Mushi.

—*Miaow!*
—Hey, Dad! Look here! A little cat—it seems to have been abandoned.
—*Miaow!*
—Say, Dad, can we take it home?
—Don't even think about it. What would your mom say?
—She'd say yes. She loves animals.

—*Miaow!*
—Look, Dad! He must be hungry. Come on, Dad! Say yes! Let's take it home!
—I won't say no, but you will have to deal with your mother, and you will need to look after this cat properly. It is not a toy.
—Oh, thank you, Dad! Come on, Minou! Come, Minou, come! Don't be afraid!
—*Miaow!*
—There! I got him! He let himself be caught!
—Then, let's go back home. Someone is in for a surprise, for sure!

—*Miaow!*
—What the heck is this?
—Mom, it is a little cat that Dad and I found when we went out for a walk. It was lost.

—And what do you intend to do with it? You should take it to the animal-rescue center.

—Oh, Mom! Can we keep it, please?

—*Miaow!*

—But he will drop hairs everywhere in the house. And who is going to clean up after him, eh?

—Mom, I will look after him very well, and I promise to help you with the cleaning.

—Yeah, I would need to see that before I believe it.

—No, no, I swear!

—Hmm. If—and I am only saying *if*—we let you keep it, you must keep your promises, and if you don't, then it's off to the rescue center without any argument. Is that agreed?

—That's agreed. Oh, thank you, Mom! Come on, cat! I will show you around your new home.

—*Miaow!*

—*Miaow!*

—I believe he is still hungry.

—No, that's enough. With all that he has already eaten, he will be sick! Did you prepare everything as I have told you? His basket and his cat litter? When he is older and used to our place, he will go by himself to do his business in the garden. Cats are very clean.

—Yes. Look! He is grooming himself! He seems content!

—Say, your beast—you should think about giving it a name, perhaps. Do we even know if it is a male or a female? With little cats, one can easily get it wrong, but I am thinking that it is a male. So let's find a male name!

—I don't know. Minou?

—That is not very original. Every second cat is called Minou. He must have a special name for himself.

—I've got an idea, Dad. We are going to call him Domino.

—Domino? Why?

—Yes. *Domino* because it is black-and-white, like the pieces of the domino game that we play sometimes. You see, he has white fur on the end of his muzzle and a white triangle on his chest and also white tips on his paws. It seems as if he has little white slippers.

—OK, let's go with Domino. It sounds good!

—Domino! Domino!

—*Miaow!*

—See? He is coming. He understood and already knows his name.

—I think that he rather knows the cat food you have in your hand.

—Say, Dad, why do cats eat mice?

—Well, they have done so for ages. It is part of the balance of nature. Cats are predators!

—Predators?

—Yes—animals that feed on another specific species and prevent them from becoming too invasive, like wolves with sheep and lions with gazelles.

—Then do all animals have predators?

—Sort of, yes, and everything is generally fine if things are kept in balance, but unfortunately, mankind is interfering with the process.

—But mankind, we are also animals, no?

—Yes, we are, but we don't want to accept that we are animals because we believe we have superior intelligence. In fact, we developed into being the predators of all the other species.

—And mankind, do we have a predator that hunts us?

—No. We are our own predator because people spend a large amount of time and intelligence on fighting and killing other people. Somebody even said, "Man is a wolf to his fellow man!"

—But, Dad, you told me that there are billions of people on earth and that they will end up killing all the animals and using all the resources.

—That is quite probable, yes. Humans can already destroy themselves all at once with all sorts of weapons. It can happen anytime. They just need to press a few buttons!

—But we—we are also humans. We don't want to kill anyone. In fact, we are saving abandoned cats.

—Individually, humans are like the other animals. They are friendly if you leave them alone, but they become aggressive when they are threatened or hungry. We are just more stupid!

—More stupid?

—Yes, more stupid. The problem is that when we get together, we seem to add to the collective stupidity instead of the collective intelligence. And the bigger the group, the worse it gets! Animals may not be as intelligent as us, but at least, they are not stupid. They just follow their instincts!

—*Miaow!*

—Look at Domino. He has finished grooming, and now he is lying like a ball of fur in his basket, and I can hear him purring! Say, Dad, why do cats purr?

—Generally, they purr when they are happy.

—And the humans, why don't they purr?

—Because they are never happy!

59

Everything the Boss Has and More!

—Good morning, Monsieur Counselor.

—Good morning, Monsieur Chèvremont. Did you prepare my program for the week?

—Yes. It is nearly done, and you will be quite busy.

—All the better! We have to win this municipality back from the opposition. To do that, we must throw ourselves into everything. So run through it with me. I am listening.

—Well, on Monday, in the morning, you have to pay a visit to the town's children's home.

—That is a curious start! Babies don't vote!

—But their parents do! We need a picture of you carrying a baby in your arms to illustrate the press release that we have already written: "Dujardin and the next generation!"

—You don't want me to give him his milk bottle, I hope? You can be sure that the little thing will puke and piss through his nappies. Maybe I should bring a spare suit and shirt, just in case?

—Don't shake him too much, that's all, and hold him properly.

—OK, I shall take care, and then?

—In the afternoon, you will go to the opening of the new municipal toilets. The mayor and a few local celebrities will be there. You will probably have the opportunity to relieve yourself in the company of the actual mayor. There are only two urinals.

198

—They are not going to take a picture when we are—

—No, but there may be some technical comments. You will have to take care of possible timing issues and that the mayor will not try to take advantage of this situation by staying for a longer time "in action."

—I see. This is a bit of *Clochemerle* (*1), but if that's the way it has to be . . . and after?

—Afterward, there will be a wine reception, and then you will go back to the main street and greet some of the shopkeepers. Don't stay too long and be ready with your stock of jokes to fill the gaps in the conversation.

—That's good. How about Tuesday?

—On Tuesday, you will visit the retirement home.

—But they are all doddery old folks in there.

—Yes, but they are still voters. Our photographer will capture you enjoying a cup of tea and cookies with them. At the end, we shall do a group photo, and you will spontaneously push some old geezer in a wheelchair. The press article for this is also ready: "Dujardin respects our elders!"

—I don't like tea, but I'll do what I need to do. After?

—You will have lunch at the high school cafeteria. You will be queuing with the students and teachers, and we shall get a picture when you are served your food tray. The teachers are on our side, so there is nothing to fear from them, and for once, they will not be on strike.

—And the afternoon?

—We have been thinking about visiting a farm. You will need a good pair of boots. We have foreseen a picture with the star of the farm, who won a major award at the last agricultural show. It is a cow called Eulalie. She is a Limousin (*2). Take care not to refer to her as a Normande (*3)! And be aware that Eulalie is not a milking cow but one bred for meat. It would be quite embarrassing if you showed that you know nothing about these things because the farmers are already not very favorable to our side. The farmer will probably invite you to have a café-Calva (*4). Go easy on the Calvados because it is a homemade brew and basically a rotgut at 60 proof!

—Whew. OK, and Wednesday?

—Wednesday is the market day. You will have to walk around the stalls, shake hands, and distribute flyers. Take care not to start with the fish merchant or the cheese man because your hands will smell of fish or old camembert. We will, of course, be taking pictures of you wandering about, but we will especially take one when you buy some green salads from the vegetable merchant. We already have the caption: "Dujardin doesn't tell salads! He eats them!"

—You find that funny, do you? Oh, whatever. Let's go on. Thursday?

—On Thursday, at midday, you will join the war veterans for a wine reception. Don't forget to salute their flag first. Compliment them on their medals and ask them to tell you how they won them. They will be delighted to tell their stories for the hundredth time. Of course, there will be a group picture with the vets and the flag. "Dujardin honors our heroes!"

—No problem. After that?

—After you leave the veterans, you will have to be at the factory exit at 1700. We have prepared a stand with some placards and tracts and a group of the party members and a banner: "Dujardin is with the working class!" The trade-union delegate will hand you his loud-hailer so you can do a little speech.

—Perfect! And if it rains?

—We will move and do the same thing in the factory's great hall.

—Sounds good. Friday?

—At this stage, Friday is quite calm, but we have been wondering about some door-to-door—a kind of postman's tour. To show that you are in touch with the environment, you will ride a bicycle with two or three of our team members. This is the "simple man close to the people" angle. No more than five minutes at each stop—just long enough for them to take selfies with you. Don't accept a drink at every stop, or you might not get very far!

—OK. Saturday?

—Saturday will be spent at the school fair—a routine job. Give handshakes, visit stalls, buy some candy floss and give it to some child, play a game of massacre, hit pyramids of cans, and play a game of fishing corks from a barrel—all the usual stuff. Of course, our photographer will be ready for whenever you will have many people around you. "Dujardin with the young ones!"

—And Sunday?

—On Sunday morning, there is the mass. But it is not our usual piece of cake. That would not be well received by our supporters. So we have arranged an "impromptu" meeting with the parish priest and some parishioners concerning the maintenance of the church and of the cemetery. We shall get a photo and a story to show that you are not sectarian. It will be published in the parish bulletin.

—And Sunday afternoon?

—Ah, there is the soccer match at the stadium. You will do the kickoff and watch the game from the stands with the supporters. Don't forget to go to the refreshment stand at halftime and at the end of the match. We will have pictures of all of these, of course. "Dujardin plays hard for our city!"

—Excellent! You have done a great job with this, Monsieur Chèvremont. If, with all of this, we are not rocking the boat a little, it is to be desperate about our fellow citizens!

—Thank you, Monsieur Dujardin, or perhaps I should call you Monsieur Future Mayor?

—No, no, please—not yet. That could bring us bad luck, but . . . argh, I think you have forgotten something.

—Forgotten something? What?

—Monsieur Chèvremont, you have forgotten the part of our electorate that belongs to the recently nationalized minorities. It is important for us to make a difference for these folks. In all the pictures you have planned and everything else, there is no black interlocutor—not even someone with a bit of color. What are they going to think about us? Quick, we have to repair that!

—That's true, but it was not intentional, believe me. Well, we can still pick some appropriate pictures from the ones taken with the public and include them in the press release, but . . . wait, I have an idea.

—Tell me.

—I will arrange a "spontaneous" encounter with the municipal staff in charge of collecting the garbage cans in the morning. These workers are almost all immigrants. They will be delighted to appear with you in our campaign publicity, but you will have to get up early as they start work at five in the morning.

—Five in the morning? And they do this every day? Well, desperate times call for desperate measures. But wait, at that early hour, it is still pitch-black during this season. How will we get a good picture? We won't even see their faces.

—No problem. Modern cameras have super flashlights. Don't worry! Now let's see which day will work best. I will have to warn them.

—What about Friday? I can even empty a bin by myself, and then the workers and I—we shall share coffee that you will have previously prepared in thermos flasks, and then, presto—a picture in action: "Dujardin respects those who do the dirty jobs!"

—Great, Monsieur Dujardin! I will get on this immediately.

—Very good, Monsieur Chèvremont. It seems that we are ready for a successful week. See you on Monday. Have a good weekend. Thank you.

—Have a good weekend too, Monsieur Dujardin!

—Well, I have to contact the garbage collectors for Friday. Oh dear, I just remembered: There is no collection on Fridays. Heck! I have to call him back. Otherwise, he will get up and freeze his balls off for nothing. I wish this election was over and for all of this to end. I'm only his assistant, but I still have to do the dirty jobs and work behind the scenes. I must have patience. My turn will come!

*1. *Clochemerle*—this book (published in 1934), which has many film and TV adaptations, is a comic work that satirizes the conflicts between Catholics and Republicans in relation to the installation of a pissoir (public urinal) near a town's church.

*2. Limousin—a breed of highly muscled beef cattle that originates from the Limousin and Marche regions of France.

*3. Normande—a breed of dairy cattle that originates from the Normandy region of northwestern France.

*4. Café-Calva—hot coffee and Calvados apple brandy.

60

Redskin No Understand!

Dedicated to the Indian chief Sitting Bull.

—I am very honored that the great chief Standing Bull has accepted this powwow in his wigwam, and I am happy to present him with the greetings of the Great White Father, who is in Washington.

—Chief Standing Bull has no Great White Father, so far he knows!

—Ah, that was a way of speaking. I—

—Chief Standing Bull now sit. Chief get tired to stay standing when much talk.

—That's fine. It will be much better to sit. I am afraid that this is going to last awhile.

—Chief Standing Bull now sitting, asking why pale face wants talking again.

—Well, you see, we have to renegotiate the terms of the last treaty about the land sharing.

—Chief Standing Bull asking why have treaty when pale face always want to change and always ask for more. Pale face have forked tongue and make fun of redskins. Standing Bull sits on treaty! Standing Bull sits on pale face's demands! Standing bull sits on bluecoats and Great White Father in Washington!

—*Dear, he is quite furious, and if he spends his time on sitting like that, I have to ask myself why they call him Standing Bull, this feathered bloke. Well, we are not out of the tepee yet!*

—Pale face speaking in his beard. Redskin no understand!

—No, no, it's nothing. I was talking to myself. Well, let's talk about serious matters now.

—*Sitting or standing, I don't care, but this Indian must understand that he is becoming quite annoying now. I have thousands of migrating pioneers to settle on his land, me.*

—Pale face still speaking in his beard. Redskin no understand!

—Pardon me. You have to say to your chief that if he agrees to relocate and go into a reservation, we will look after him very well. We have prepared a tepee with three rooms, a kitchen-bathing room, and a view of the municipal landfill. So can we agree and smoke the peace pipe?

—Chief Standing Bull stop smoking. Smoking not good for redskin lungs.

—Then, if he does not smoke, what about a case of whiskey?

—Chief Standing Bull stop booze. Booze not good for redskin liver.

—Then, why not a few pills and syringes that make some nice dreams?

—Chief Standing Bull stop chemical shit. Dope not good for redskin brain.

—*That's all we needed! How can we get rid of him now?*

—Pale face talking again in his beard. Redskin no understand!

—Well, it's nothing. I was just thinking. How about we give him some nice glass jewelry for his squaws and toys and sweets for his papooses and have a group picture?

—Chief Standing Bull say stop taking him for an idiot. He not want move house and go reservation. He wants rifles to hunt buffalos!

—But there are no more buffalos, not even in a can!

—Then Chief Standing Bull hunt pale faces! Sick of pale faces. Pale faces stealing hunting grounds. Pale faces kill all buffalos. Pale faces coming with bullshit religion. Manitou not happy! Pale faces destroy customs of redskins, bring fucking illnesses, rape squaws!

—*Well, the least one can say now is that the negotiation has failed. Anyways, it was only for the principle. One cannot stop history. This guy is doomed!*

—Pale face always talking in his beard. Redskin tired of no understand!

—No, I was saying to the chief that finally, it is no use to renegotiate the treaty. But why is he laughing, this old bugger?

—Standing Bull have fun because before powwow, he speaking with medicine man to know future.

—So what?

—And then, medicine man say redskin is screwed but pale face also screwed!

—What?

—Yes, medicine man say he sees many more men coming—all colors: yellow, black, and also little green men. Pale face forced to sign treaty or go to reservation!

—*No, but what? He is making fun of me, this lousy Indian!*

—Pale face no understand why redskin laughing under his feathers? Ha ha! Pale face will understand later! Too late!

61

Underground Music!
Dedicated to Sven.

—Hey! What the hell are you doing here?

—Well, as you can see, I am playing the violin!

—Yes, but do you have authorization to play in this station?

—No! Why? Since when do I need authorization?

—Since I told you. This station is part of our territory.

—But what do you mean? We are in France. We are free to do as we like, no?

—Yes, you are free, but you have to pay for our protection. You pay and you can stay. You don't pay and you fuck off or you will have problems. A violin is quite fragile, no?

—But I cannot pay. Me, I have no money. If I had money, do you think I would be here and passing the hat? I am doing this to pay for my study. I don't have a bourse (*1).

—No bourse? Just my luck to come upon one without gender (*1).

—No, I am not without my bits. I did not get a student bourse. And I must manage by myself.

—Ah, Monsieur is studying! And what are you studying, if you don't mind me asking?

—I am trying to earn a license in anthropology and paleontology.

—What?

—I am studying fossils.

—Fake eyelashes (*2)? You don't look like a drag queen either! But one can be wrong.

—No, *fossils*. There are bones or pieces of debris that can be thousands of years old—sometimes even millions!

—And you are playing music for that? I was thinking that your music was a bit old-fashioned. What is it that you are playing?

—It is classical music. Beethoven, Vivaldi, Strauss—

—Never heard about those guys. Never seen them on TV or social media!

—They were great composers, but they have been dead for a long time.

—Probably contemporaries of the bones you are studying. Well, we are not here to talk about music or whatever you said you were studying. You pay or you don't pay! It is thirty euros a day.

—Could you give me credit until this evening? So I have time to collect a bit of money?

—And you will disappear! I have already heard that one before! I know the music too!

—If it's going to be like that, then I'll just have to move to another station.

—Wait! Hold on! We will think of something. You see, I quite like students. If they did not hold those demonstrations, we would not be able to go out from time to time and break a few shop windows when the cops are busy with fighting them. I have a little deal to propose.

—OK, I am listening.

—You stay here and scratch your thing, but I will leave you with a little bag with some sachets that some guys will come to collect. They will use a password—let's say, "Vive Aldi [*3]." Ha ha, you will like that one. They will lean over as if to drop a coin in your violin box, but in fact, they will pick up one of the sachets hidden inside. You will keep playing without seeming to notice. You see? This will be easy. Nobody will suspect anything.

—In short, you want to recruit me as an accomplice. Is that right?

—But no, not accomplice—just a little service to pay for your thirty euros.

—Yes, but with this trick, you will have nothing on yourself, and I shall be the one at risk of being caught with your dope if the police catch on.

—You don't need to worry about the police, mate. We also have a deal with them so that they are not too zealous. We leave them in peace, and they leave us alone, and everybody is happy! There is only the drug-dog patrol that we cannot control, and those damned beasts can sniff out the weed from miles away. By luck, they don't venture very often to the underground. But if you are that concerned, you could just keep a few of your fossils in your pockets and say that the pooch must have been attracted to them. Ha ha, the look on the faces of the cops—I would like to see that!

—Yeah, well . . . OK, we can give it a go, I guess. But I don't want to end up playing violin in the jail (*4).

—That would be funny, ha ha!

—I don't find it so funny!

—Well, anyways, you have made the right choice, buddy. You will see—we will be doing business together, and you will raise your study money in no time. Here is the bag with the sachets. I'll put it under this handkerchief in your violin case. Now you can start playing the game. By the way, what's the name of that piece you were just playing?

—"A Little Night Music"—it is from Mozart!

—Ah! Now, if you want my opinion, you should try playing the guitar! OK, get on with it. I'll see you this evening!

*1. *Bourse* (scholarship): In French, the same word can mean "scholarship" and also "testicles." Therefore, the intentional confusion is possible.

*2. *Fossiles* (fossils) also sounds like *faux cils* (false eyelashes), therefore the intentional confusion and drag-queen joke are possible.

*3. Vivaldi (Italian composer) and "Vive Aldi" (Long life to Aldi) build an instance of wordplay.

*4. *Violon* (violin): In French, it means the musical instrument, but it is also used as a slang word for "jail."

62

The Blind and the Paralytic!
Dedicated to Sarah.

—Pray, my beloved brothers and sisters! Pray! Let's praise the Almighty Lord together. Lord, we are your humble servants. Show us your way. Give us the strength to follow it and overcome all the obstacles of the physical life. God, we aspire to the eternal life. Spare us the temptations of the devil, this monster gone out of hell to lead us astray. Pray, my beloved brothers and sisters, and God will show himself in all his glory, his might, and his mercy. Pray! God is with us now. I feel his warmth in me, his messenger. God talks with my voice and acts with my hands. Pray and open your eyes and your hearts.

—Look at the poor wretch who is now coming toward me. Look at him closely because he is possessed by the demon. Look at his bulging eyes and the dribble coming out of his mouth. See the convulsions shaking his limbs. This is what happens to those who don't welcome God. See the diabolical work of Satan. You there, miserable one, come! Come and you will be saved if you believe in HIM!

—ARGH!

—Do YOU believe in God, our Lord?

—ARGH . . . YES!

—Louder! Say, "I believe in you, God. Deliver me from the evil occupying my body!"

—ARGH! I BELIEVE IN GOD! YES! I believe. Please deliver me from evil!

—That's good. Pray, my beloved brothers and sisters, and now, WATCH! Open your mouth, you! Open wide! That's it. I see it. I see the devil. I see the snake—the same one that damned Adam and Eve. I see its filthy head. With the power of God that is in me, I am going to rip the devil out of your body! I am holding it! Here it is! It is coming! And it is going out of your body through your mouth!

—ARGH!

—Do you see it now, wriggling in my hand? My brothers and sisters, do you see it at the end of my arm? Lucifer has gone out of the body of this man! Now go in peace and praise the Lord. My beloved brothers and sisters, let's pray together and thank God for this miracle.

—And now, look at who is coming toward me. Look at who is begging for God's mercy. Who are you? And why are you pushing this other man in a wheelchair? Are you coming for him?

—No, not only him. It is for him and for me too. He, he is a paralytic, and me, I am blind. So I push him, and he tells me where to go.

—My beloved brothers and sisters, what a lesson of helping each other, truthfully! Certainly, it is God who sent them to us today, and it is God who is going to reward them! You two, do you believe in God? Do you believe in his mercy and power?

—YES, WE DO BELIEVE IN GOD ALMIGHTY!

—Then, my friends, pray with me! Lord, I beseech you. I am appealing to your mercy for these two poor men who believe in you and who have been so badly struck by misery. God Almighty, give them another chance. For you, the blind, let there be light. Open your eyes! I order you! God Himself orders you! Come on! OPEN YOUR EYES AND SEE!

—AH! AH! My eyes, they burn! AH! The light is burning my eyes! AH! But what is this? It's like blinkers are moving! AH! I CAN SEE! I CAN SEE!

—Yes, you see, and you can glorify the Lord, who has done this miracle. My beloved brothers and sisters, let's glorify God and pray with this man. Praise be the Lord! Our Lord!

And now, you, sitting there in the chair—did you not feel the power of God Almighty? If YOU believe in HIM, he will give it back a hundredfold!

—I feel some warmth and tingling in my legs. It is bizarre!

—My beloved brothers and sisters, we also have to pray for this man so that he can be freed from his misery. Let's BELIEVE and PRAY!

—AH! My legs!

—Come on! If you believe in HIM, stand up! I command you!

—I am afraid!

—STAND UP AND WALK!

—I am going to fall! Help me!

—No! Help yourself, and God will help you! STAND UP! There we go. See? Don't tremble like that. God is with you. We are all with you. And now, WALK! Here. One step. Two steps. You are walking! You can even get on your knees with all of us to thank God for having pity on you and on your friend. And you, my beloved brothers and sisters, you can go home now in the peace of God. Be the witnesses of what you have seen today and spread the word of God around you!

—Well, now it's finished! Is everybody gone?

—Yes. There is only the four of us left. Everything has gone well this time again. How much did we make tonight?

—Somewhere around fifty thousand. The entry tickets plus the merchandising: T-shirts, caps, crosses, etc. I have not yet counted the holy water but all the cash here down on the ground in the bag.

—That's not too bad for a godforsaken place like this town! Don't forget to refill the bottles at the tap for the next show. Everybody played his part well—even our old Lucifer. This old toothless snake actually loves it when I keep him warm in my sleeve and pull him out as if he is coming out of your mouth. It is really spectacular. As for the rest, the act of the blind and the paralytic is running quite well, but don't forget to change your appearances so you won't be recognized at the next show. Anyways, we are going to the other side of the country on my private jet. Come on, let's pack up and go.

—Hey! What happened? It looks like a power outage.

—No, it's nothing. It is already on again.

—But no, it is not on. It is not the same light. It seems to come from nowhere.

—Probably the security system. Never mind. As long as we can see something.

—Hey, look there! That bloody Lucifer used the opportunity to get out of his bag, and it is running around on the ground.

—Wait, I am going to get him back. Lucifer, come here!

—WATCH OUT! That is not Lucifer! It's a real—

—AH! Too late! He bit me!

—AH! It is hurting bad! It burns! And I feel a coldness climbing up my leg!

—Wait. Lie there on the ground. Stay still to slow down the progress of the venom. We'll call for help.

—There is no need!

—Why?

—That thing is a minute snake. Their bites are almost always fatal. He has only thirty seconds left!

—AH! My eyes are burning! I cannot see! AH! My body is so cold!

—AH!

—Now it is done! He is dead! One minute flat!

—Shit! What are we going to do now?

—Let's leave him there and run away with the money!

—Wait. This light, it is quite bizarre indeed. It's as if somebody is watching us.

—An even better reason to light a shuck!

—Hey! What's happening to me? I cannot feel my legs. They are getting numb. Hand me the wheelchair so that I can sit in it for a while.

—Yes, but where is it? I cannot see it!

—It's right in front of you.

—Hey! My view is blurred! I can hardly see you!

—What is going on with the two of you? If it is a game, it is not funny! Come on! I am going to pick up that money bag, and we are getting the hell out of here!

—I cannot move! I am paralyzed!

—I cannot see! I am blind!

—Is that so? Then, sorry, mates, but you can fend for yourselves. The sharing will be easier! Ha ha! All the fucking money will be for me! Adios!

—Bastard! Motherfucker! Asshole! The devil drop you dead!

—AH!

—What is it now?

—That damned snake! It was hidden in the pile of money! When I picked up the bag, it bit me! AH!

—Ha! So the tables have turned! We can start the stopwatch. One minute—just enough time for a little prayer!

—AH!

—He is dead! He didn't even last a minute!

—Well, now there are only the two of us left. Push my chair and let's get outta here! I shall guide you!

—But what about the dough?

—Leave it! That is Satan's money!

63

Strategy!

—Hey! Sergeant, where are we now?

—I have no idea! Somewhere in the north of France. But because they have taken out all the road signs to confuse the enemy, we too don't know where we are—even with a map. Look at the captain. He seems to be lost as well!

—And where are we going anyways?

—I have no idea. Toward the south, for sure. It's a strategic retreat!

—A strategic retreat?

—Yes! You go back to prepared-in-advance positions, and when the enemy is tired of running after you, you throw a counterattack!

—Ah, good! That's a great strategy! But what do we do in the meantime?

—We camp in that little wood over there on the hill—away from the main road. So if the Germans come down this road, there is a good chance that they will pass by without even noticing us. Anyway, the captain said that we had to hold the position but we are not here to be overzealous!

—What does that mean, "Hold the position"? The place is not going to move.

—No, it is another strategic term.

—Again?

—Yes, but I do believe that it will be us who will be going to move and rather fast. We spend the night there, and early in the morning, we move out quickly before Fritz (*1) brings us breakfast!

—And the rest of the regiment, where is it?

—No idea! Probably further south. They had a few vehicles left, and they were going faster than us.

—And the Germans? They have tanks, the panzers, and we—where are our tanks?

—No idea! But our generals probably know that. This is the strategy again.

—I hope they do! The generals, in a time of peace, you see plenty of them. But where are they now?

—Much further south, I guess. They are probably experimenting with the strategic withdrawal by themselves.

—Ah, good! But the Germans there, they also have plenty of planes— the Stukas and the Messerschmitts. Our planes, where the hell are they?

—They are probably with our tanks. All of this has been thought out in advance. The Germans will fall into the trap. They—they have no idea about strategy. They are just dense brutes who make war by charging forward without thinking. They do the same when they play soccer!

—Yes, but with soccer, they are quite successful, no?

—Well, guys, that's not all. What about a little casse croute (*2)?

—Good idea. What do we have?

—Everything we need. By luck, you'd have to say that we are pretty well set up when it comes to food. The quality of the grub is the real nerve of the war. Here, we have fresh bread, and we still have plenty of sausages and cheese. And concerning the wine, we have enough ammunition to fight another war!

—Yeah. At least, it will be as much as the Germans will not get. Ha ha!

—And if this isn't strategy, I know nothing about it!

*1. *Fritz*—nickname used to refer to German soldiers.
*2. *Casse croûte*—a solid snack that usually consists of bread, cheese, dry sausage, and wine.

64

Whose Fault Is It?

—Hey! Did you see the article in the newspaper? About the two guys who drove into a plane tree while trying to escape from the police with a stolen car? Two dead! It is not a pity to see this sort of thing! And whose fault is it, yeah?

—For sure, this will be seen as the police's fault. The story is already written. White march, petition, newspaper articles, cars set on fire, and the rest of the usual circus! Nowadays, it is the little suburban scums who are dictating the laws. Soon, the thieves will run after the policemen and catch them! Yeah, they always benefit from attenuating circumstances. First, they are too young, and it gives them the right to do silly things. Then, it's not their fault. It is society's fault for failing to integrate them properly and teach them good manners!

—Yeah! It is the fault of our education system. They had been expelled. How stupid also to try to teach them things that they don't care about: calculus, national language, spelling, history, geography, sciences, and all the like. Only garbage that they do not need! And I am not even talking about civic responsibilities or morality. Nowadays, those are notions that just make people laugh!

—Yeah! It is not just the fault of the school programs but also the fault of the teachers, no? In the old days, we had real teachers—well trained and effective. Now it is only a job left for those who have not been able to do anything better. They do it just to get holidays and job security. And there's no need to talk about discipline and respect. Those went into oblivion a long time ago!

—The teachers, I agree, but you should start looking at the parents too. They lay children like eggs without being able to look after them properly. It's the street and the buddies who are in charge of their education. And what are they learning? The parents—they content themselves with pocketing the social-welfare benefits or punching a teacher when one was courageous enough to blame their dirty brat for misbehaving!

—Me, I think it is the fault of these stupid movies and video games. There are only showing crimes, gunfights, explosions, brawls, unrealistic car pursuits, and so-called superheroes to normalize all the violence. What sort of example is it to follow for those kids who only have peas for brains!

—Wait! You just forgot that it is firstly the fault of the owner of the stolen car, no? What was he thinking, that idiot, to leave his car door unlocked with the key in the ignition when he just popped into the store to buy a pack of cigarettes? If you own one of those flashy big German cars, you should be a little more careful. It is the opportunity that makes the thief. If he had only locked the door, we would not be in this situation now!
—And buying cigarettes? Here we are again—all of this because of the bloody smoking! If that idiot had not been a smoker, those two kids would still be alive. Double fault for him!

—That's not all. Have you ever noticed the road where the accident happened? The bend is too sharp and comes just after a straight line where you can speed without even noticing it. It is not properly signposted, and you can be surprised. Then, it just needs a few loose pieces of gravel lying around, and then *wham*! You hit the tree! It is the fault of the road services and of the administration!
—Yes, but you can manage that bend safely at 80 without a problem! But when you are at 150 or 180, even with a good car, that is another story!

—What a stupid thing also to build cars that can go so fast when the speed is limited everywhere now! It is the fault of the car manufacturers! There should be a law against them!

—Well, ladies and gentlemen of the city council, thank you for expressing your minds on this painful subject. Now, my view as the mayor of this city is that we have to show the people that we are doing something. They are calling for positive actions, so let's act. As a first step, while we wait for the emotion to fade and the public opinion to be busy with something else, what would you suggest by way of concrete propositions? Monsieur Deputy Mayor?

—Well . . . um . . .

—City Counselors?

—Well . . . um . . .

—Members of the opposition? You are welcome to speak.

—Well . . . um . . .

—Monsieur Mayor? Please, could I say something?

—Monsieur Lagenais, you are not a member of the council, but yes, the opinion of a fellow citizen can be useful. What would you like to share?

—Well, Monsieur Mayor, I was listening to you while repairing this electrical switch, as it is my job. It's all very well, what has been said, but I think you have forgotten that, before anything else, it is the fault of those two young thugs, who were raising havoc in the suburb where I happen to live myself. It is certainly very regrettable, what has happened to them, but they were asking for trouble and now will be no worse off. Personally, I believe that a few kicks in the ass that are given at the right time and for the right reasons would have had more impact on their careers than soothing blah-blah when it is too late, and that would have saved their lives!

—I thank you, Monsieur Lagenais, for this rather rude way of putting things, but you will understand that I cannot spend my time kicking the bottoms of some of my fellow citizens and of their offspring. We must find another way.

—Monsieur Mayor, we have forgotten another culprit!

—Ah yes, and which one?

—The tree, Monsieur Mayor, the tree! If it had not been there, there would not have been such a crash and not these two fatalities!

—For heaven's sake, of course, yes! This is the tree's fault! Why is it growing there anyways?

—But, Monsieur Mayor, it is an old tree. It has always been there. In summer, people like to have a picnic in its shade.

—Ah, my dear colleague, it's nearly as if Brassens is talking to us: "Close to my tree, I was living happy!" (*1)

—Ah, Brassens—another time! We remember when we were young—isn't that so, Monsieur Mayor?

—Yes, memories of our youth, maybe, but at the moment, the safety of the youth in our city is most important. Tomorrow, Monsieur Deputy Mayor, you will see our chief of the municipal services and ask him to send a team with chainsaws to cut down that tree. Make sure to inform the press before starting anything, and I will pay a visit myself and be there to be in the picture.

—But what about the greenies? They will not like it, those tree huggers!

—To hell with the environmentalists! We will plant another tree for them somewhere else! Ladies and gentlemen, the matter is settled. The session is adjourned. Thank you and have a good evening!

*1. Georges Brassens (1921–1981)—a famous French poet and singer.

65

A Bag of Marbles!

—Hey! Come with me and play marbles!

—OK. What game are we going to play?

—Your choice! The triangle (*1), the pursuit (*2), the line (*3), or the pyramid (*4).

—Let's go for the line so that others can join us. Come on!

—Holy cow! You have won all my marbles! I am not going to play with you again. You are too good! Give me some back!

—Too bad for you, mate. You should not have played. The bell is ringing. We have to get back to our classroom.

—What is that noise? A marble rolling on the classroom floor! Who does it belong to?

—Miss, Miss, it's Pierrot's! He was counting his marbles in his bag!

—Pierrot, bring me that bag!

—But, Madam, I—

—I told you one hundred times that I don't want marbles in the classroom. I am going to confiscate this bag and will only give it back at the recreation if you are working well. Come on, give it to me!

—Well, children, lay down your pencils. You can go out for the recreation. In order, please! Here, Pierrot, your bag, but don't do this again, understood?

—Yes, Miss! Thank you, Miss!

—You dirty tattler! You denounced me! Here is something for your face!

—Ah, my nose! It is bleeding! You big brute! I am going to tell the teacher, you will see! Miss, Miss! He hit me!

—What is this again? Stop fighting like cats and dogs! You again, Pierrot? I've had enough of you two. Come, you will spend the rest of the recreation standing here with your hands on your heads. That will calm you both down when you should have been playing with marbles peacefully like the others!

—Monsieur General Secretary of the United Nations, bravo for your speech on the proliferation of nuclear weapons. You were warmly applauded.

—Yes. Alas, that was only a speech, and I doubt that the countries we are most concerned about will learn any lesson and change. We don't have the power to sanction them.

—Yes, and they are too preoccupied with counting their warheads like schoolboys counting their marbles, and they are only thinking about playing with them!

—If, at least, we could confiscate them and prevent the countries from fighting like naughty boys, we could have a bit of peace in this world of madmen!

*1. Triangle—the aim is to knock marbles set inside a triangle drawn in the dust. If they go out, you win them.
*2. Pursuit—hit the opponent's marbles one at a time to win them or keep going from where the marble has stopped rolling.
*3. Line—each throws a marble as close as possible to a line drawn on the ground. The closest one wins the marbles of the other players.
*4. Pyramid—set up a pyramid of four or more marbles. Standing from a line a few meters away, the other players will try to break the pyramid. The marbles that miss will belong to the setter, and all the pyramid marbles are won by the thrower when they score a hit.

66

Test-Tube Babies!

—And, my dear colleagues, I will now conclude this presentation with a look into the future. With the ongoing experiments, we have some good reasons to believe that we will see some significant progress in the coming years. The improvement of our cultivation techniques, the selection of the cells and embryos, and the development of the stem cells can allow us to imagine results that will considerably change our concepts of not only animal but also human reproduction. Of course, the ethical aspects of our experiments cannot be set aside and will probably require some adaptations of the existing legislation. But if we don't do it, others will do it in our place with consequences that you can guess concerning the political and commercial repercussions. Our duty, as scientists, is to go always further in our searches and leave to others the responsibilities incumbent to them. Ladies and gentlemen, I thank you for your attention!

—Please, Monsieur Professor, do you have a moment for me?
—Yes. What is going on?
—Well, there is something bizarre happening that I would like to show you. Can you come with me to the laboratory?
—Let's go. I will follow you.
—Here. See the trays we are using for our cell cultures. In tray 7, there are abnormal developments. I have collected a sample for you to look at with the microscope. There, see for yourself!

—Yes, you are right! What the hell is that?

—You see the cell here in the center. Its composition is different. And what is more, when you observe it for a while, you will see that it seems to be killing the other cells by feeding on them!

—But this is absolutely incredible! What you are telling me?

—Well, it does not kill them but rather assimilate them. Check its composition, and you will find all the characteristics of the assimilated cells!

—This is fabulous! It looks like a super cell!

—Yes, but the problem is that we do not know how these cells could have come into contact with each other because normally, they are placed in different test tubes. We have not only samples of diverse animal origins but also human ones.

—That's right. This should never have happened unless somebody involuntarily or accidentally mixed them. Are you sure that you have strictly followed our protocols?

—Monsieur Professor! You know me! If I had made a handling error, I would have let you know immediately.

—I don't doubt that for one second! But besides you and me, nobody is allowed to enter this laboratory, which is classified as top secret. The doors only open with a secret password.

—But, Monsieur Professor, there could be only one other possibility: There is also a servicewoman who comes every day to clean up and empty the bins.

—So you are suggesting that—

—Well, we'd better talk with her for sure.

—That's good. Go and find her. We have to get this sorted out.

—Well, Germaine, I would like to ask you a few questions. I do not need to tell you how important this matter is, so please leave nothing out when you are answering me.

—Of course. As you wish, Monsieur Professor.

—First, during your activities in this laboratory, did you happen to touch any of the samples that are staying there?

—Oh, Monsieur Professor, I am too afraid of those things to do that. All the bizarre stuff in the jars—some of them look like fetuses. It is terrible and gives me nightmares.

—Yes, Germaine, I can understand that, but you have to tell me the truth. I assure you that even if something had happened, you will not be criticized or reprimanded. It will stay between us.

—Well, um . . . then . . . OK. The other day, when I was sweeping under a table, my broom handle bumped against one of the trays, and some tubes tipped over and what was in them spilled onto the tray!

—That can happen to anybody, but then, what did you do?

—Well, all the contents of the tubes made a mess on the bottom of the tray. So very carefully, with a spoon, I ladled it back into the tubes, and I also transferred a bit of liquid from some tubes of the nearby trays to top up the tubes—to make it look like nothing had happened. And then I cleaned the tray. I'm sorry. I was so afraid that I might lose my job.

—Very well, Germaine. Thank you for being honest, and I assure you that you will not lose your job. Can you remember which tray it was and from which tubes you used liquid to top them up?

—Yes, it was this tray here, number 7, and I took the liquid from the nearby tray over there, number 6.

—It's good that you can remember them. And when did it happen?

—About two weeks ago, maybe a bit more.

—That's fine. Thank you. You can go now and get on with your work. I assure you that nothing really grave happened. In a way, you may even have helped us. Thank you for your time.

—Thank you, Monsieur Professor. I am so sorry. It was just an accident. I got afraid, and—

—Don't worry! Please don't! And away you can go.

—So, Monsieur Professor?

—So, my dear friend, we have just made a scientific discovery of the highest importance. It is as simple as that!

—But what shall we do with these samples that have been mixed? We should be destroying them. If not, they will falsify our research!

—Don't even think about it! On the contrary, you will look after these samples as if they are the apple of your eyes. And we will continue as if nothing happened.

—But the embryos and these cells will develop! And we have no idea what will be produced!

—No, we don't know, but we shall see, and we shall know!

—I am a bit afraid, Professor. What if we are creating mutants or monsters?

—But are we, humans, not already mutants and monsters?

67

When the Music is Good

—We now have to choose the candidate who will represent France in the next Eurovision Song Contest (*1). You already know about the situation. We have to admit that in recent years, we have not done well and sometimes have even been ridiculous. The public opinion and social media are accusing us of nominating mediocre contenders, and they are making fun of us.

—Yeah, but who cares about the public opinion? They know nothing. All they want is a good-looking female singer with a nice song in the pure tradition of French singing. What they want is out of fashion!
—Yes, maybe, but people have also had enough of these so-called singers who are more or less unknown and who will soon disappear!
—They are stupid fools! We are here to educate them and show them what true artists really are.
—Ah, is that so? And what are true artists like?
—Well, they are modern. Yes, that's it—they represent modern ideas!

—Yes, but if you want my advice, it does not change the fact that to have a good song, you need a good melody, good music, attractive lyrics, poetry, romanticism—things that people can identify with!
—On the contrary, you have to punch them in the face and blow them away with sex, provocation, bizarre outfits and behaviors, aggressive words, and dancers all over the place. Make it a show! That's the way!

—Yeah, the more dancers there are, the less you are likely to hear the singer, and most of the time, that will be preferable!

—I see that we are not on the same artistic line and will never agree. But let's see the candidates who were selected during the first audition. Maybe there will be one who will make unanimity. What are your propositions?

—Well, we have Carole. She is a real looker, and she dances well—

—I thought this was a singing contest? The poor gal has no voice, and apart from wiggling her bottom rhythmically, I cannot see what we could do with her.

—We also have Lamal.

—Who the hell is that? I have never heard the name!

—He is a young guy and a bit asocial. We found him singing in the underground.

—And that is supposed to be a reference? Another one of those guitar scratchers, I suppose.

—Yes. He writes lyrics and sets them to the music he composes. With a good backing band and proper staging, he could do the job.

—But the lyrics, even if they are good, will not do the job. The other countries will not understand a word of what he is singing. Nowadays, everybody sings in English!

—Then, why not a duo? We have Pierrot Pierrette. They are brother and sister. They fit well together and have good voices.

—Yes, but it might smell a bit sappy, no? Who else do we have?

—There is Kamaz—an immigrant of Turkish background. He has good percussions and an oriental sound.

—Good on him, but it will seem a bit bizarre to have him represent France, no? And I don't think that the Turkish representative will be performing a French song.

—Then, why not the Chenapans (*2)? It is a three-guy group that is doing well with suburban rap. It is pretty hot and rough. Young people tend to like that.

—Is that the sort who is saying "We should kill the cops!"?

—No, they just want to bash them!

—Then, the opinion will not be swallowed too well. It is out of the question for the moment!

—We are left with Mistigri—a little pretty chick who is still a teenager. A bit of a Barbie doll!

—You want to reproduce the coup of France Gall (*3), but that is out of fashion now.

—Me, I am for Joselina. She is a transgender with a beard and a mustache, and she dresses as a woman and sings with a woman's voice.

—That has already been done. We will be seen as trying to copy.

—We could perhaps find an artist who is already well-known and popular and who would accept the job.

—Not a chance. Those people are well aware that they have everything to lose if they fail.

—So we have not gotten very far. We have to make a choice. But how do we do that? Should we vote? Little papers or lifted hands?

—Papers! A bit of secrecy could be perhaps preferable.

—Good, let's do it. Write the name of your champion and give me the papers.

—Thank you. Now here are the results.

—France one point. France un point. Frankreich ein punkt. (*3)

—Ah! Sorry, I got confused. It's the force of habit, you know!

*1. Eurovision Song Contest is a yearly singing competition between fifty countries that are mostly European.

*2. *chenapans* (rascals)

*3. France Gall—one of the last French singers to win the Eurovision (1965) with the song "Poupée de cire, poupée de son" when she was only seventeen.

*4. "France one point . . ."—the boring and ridiculous way to call the results of the judges of the Eurovision, which has become a standard for TV stupidity.

68

No Age for the Braves!

—Good morning, Doctor.

—Good morning, Monsieur Strongiron. How are you doing?

—If it was really good, I would not be here!

—I guess so, but more precisely? You have some pain? A fever? I need symptoms.

—I feel rusty. Ah, Doctor, I see that you are smiling. Yes, I know. "Iron-Rusted"—that joke has been following me since primary school. But one cannot choose their patronym.

—There is also "Iron-Health"—that would be preferable, but finish with the jokes. Tell me everything.

—Well, um, I have some difficulties concerning the, um, the thing!

—At your age, that is not surprising, you know, especially after you turn sixty.

—Yes, I know, but so far, it was working quite well. A bit like the leech, as people used to say—white hairs but a green tail (*1).

—Yes, I know it. But now you are at which vegetable?

—Well, I am becoming an old pickle, if you believe my wife!

—Must I understand that you are not satisfying her anymore?

—Well, you know how it goes. At first, there is fire, then there comes a time when you start to get a bit consumed and you need to refuel yourself. There are some obligations that you have to fill.

—So you would like what? Some stimulants? You know, there are now some quite-efficient medications for these sorts of things. You take a little blue pill, and there it goes again, like in '14—bayonet at the ready (*2). Of course, you must not abuse the thing, or you would be burning the candle from both sides, but it will help in case of a breakdown.

—Is that refunded by the social assistance?

—Probably if you have a doctor's prescription.

—Well, OK. Let's do the prescription.

—Here it is. Take your paper and keep me informed on the results.

—Thank you, Doctor. Goodbye. Have a good day.

—Good morning, Madam . . . so, Strongiron is your name, I see.

—Yes. Good morning, Doctor.

—Strongiron? I know that name. But you are very young. I should have said *Miss*, then? Are you related to one of my patients of the same name? His daughter, maybe?

—No, I am his wife!

—His wife? Ah, I understand better now.

—You understand what?

—No, nothing. Excuse me. I was just talking to myself. Well, what can I do now for you, Madam?

*1. "Green tail [queue verte]"—a popular French way to call the male instrument.
*2. "Like in '14"—like during World War 1

69

Lifting of the Colors

—Section, in line! I want to see only one head! Stand up! Still! At ease! That's good. Today, as a part of your basic training, you will have to perform an exercise of visual maneuvring in semi-open ground. While figuring out a situation without radio communication, you will have to reach a target destination and follow the directions that will be given with a set of colored flags. Understood?

—YES, SERGEANT!

—There will be five different colors: green means "Move forward," red means "Stop," blue means "Move backward," white means "Turn left," and yellow means "Turn right." Understood?

—YES, SERGEANT!

—Well now, to check if you have really understood, is there some little smart-ass in your platoon who will be able to tell me what you have to do if I lift the green and the yellow flags simultaneously? I am waiting!

—Yes, Serg. I have understood. We would have to move forward and turn right!

—Bravo! What is your name?

—Santin, Serg!

—Good, Second Class Santin. You will lead this group of recruits. You have the makings of a corporal, at least! So, all of you, you have understood now?

—YES, SERGEANT!

—You there, the tall guy! You will serve as the visual relay. You will stand a hundred meters away from me and also a hundred meters away from the maneuvring platoon. Then from two hundred meters away, I will guide the platoon to follow the appropriate way to the objective. You, the relay guy—all you will have to do is watch me with your field glasses and see which flag I am lifting, and then you raise the flag with the same color for your comrades. Understood?

—Yes, Sergeant, but—

—Did I hear something? "BUT"? Have you not been told that you should not discuss the orders of a superior? There is no BUT!

—Yes, Sergeant! But—

—What? Again? Who do you think you are, and where are you from?

—Sergeant, I am a daltonien (*1).

—So what? What does it matter? Daltonian, Dalmatian, Estonian, etc.—we are all part of the foreign legion, no? And it is the same for everybody. Go. Take your flags and go to your assigned post of visual relay. That's an order!

—Yes, Serg!

—Sergeant?

—Yes, Captain?

—I watched your visual-control exercise with the new recruits. It was a disaster! The platoon marched all over the place and did not make it to the objective.

—Alas, yes, sir. I don't know what happened. Usually, it works quite well.

—It seemed to me that there was a problem at the visual-relay stage of the operation, no?

—Yes, it was that idiot of a Dalmatian or Daltonian or whatever he is. I don't know exactly where he comes from. He understood nothing and was pretty useless!

—Sergeant, did I hear you say *daltonien*?

—Yes, but I am not sure if I got that one right. I have no idea where his bloody country is on the map! Never set my feet there, anyways.

—Do you know what a daltonien is, Sergeant? Obviously not. That's a guy who is color-blind. He sees everything in different shades of white, gray, and black—a bit like the old pictures in black-and-white.

—But . . . that idiot, he should have said something!

—So, Sergeant, you will have to do this drill again tomorrow. Be sure that you choose better next time.

—Yes, Captain.

—That's just my luck! What can I do, me, if this bloody army is recruiting half-blind guys who are not even able to lift a flag properly? Estonian, Dalmatian, Algerian, Daltonian—are they not all the same so long as they can carry a rifle? Next time, they will probably pick all the deaf and dumb guys from this area and ask me to make radio operators out of them. What a bloody mess! It is no surprise that we have not been able to win a proper war for ages!

70

Encounter of the Third Kind

—Hey! What's wrong with Leopold? He is running as if he had the devil on his tail. Ho! Leopold, what happened to you?

—Ah, my friends, this is terrible! I saw them!

—You saw them? Who?

—The aliens, of course! Right down the lane and in my field! They have come, I tell you! I saw them!

—Come on, Leopold. Calm down a bit. Aliens do not exist. They are things invented by the news media for suckers and Hollywood for science-fiction movies.

—Yes, but . . . the blinding light, the flying saucer, the creatures with the long arms—I saw them all!

—OK, OK, you saw them. But you should start by telling us everything from the beginning. Here, have a drink before you tell the story. It will help you recover.

—You see, I was down in the valley, in my potato-and-cabbage field, and I was just finishing up the day, doing a last inspection before coming back to the village before nightfall. Suddenly, I heard a bizarre noise, a sort of whistling, and then all at once, everything was illuminated by a blinding light that came from behind the hedge that separates my field from the next one—as if it had just fallen from the sky!

—Then what did you do?

—I was terrified! I ran to hide myself behind my old garden toolshed. Then I tried to look through the gaps between the planks.

—And what did you see?

—Two shapes appeared. The blinding light was coming from behind them, so they looked completely black, and it was impossible to see the details of their faces. I could only see that they had immensely long arms, like claws.

—And then?

—Then—well, they did not notice me, and they moved toward the thicket in the corner of the field and disappeared. I did not dare to move because there was always the light and the whistling noise, and I was afraid that they would come back and find me.

—And did they come back?

—Yes! And they were holding two rabbits, which were struggling in their hands. I thought they were trying to talk to them or trying to make them talk. Anyways, they went toward the light with their captives, and a moment later, everything went black, and then nothing!

—This seems curious indeed. If they really were aliens, do you think they could have mistaken the rabbits, which are numerous around there, for the main inhabitants of this planet? And they wanted to capture a couple?

—Me, I would rather think that Leopold has been abusing the rotgut that he makes for himself, and God only knows what its ingredients are!

—No, I swear I was not loaded! Not more than usual, anyway. I don't have any of that stuff left, and I must brew some more.

—Yeah? A drunkard's oath! How can we believe it? You can smell the stale drink from a mile away!

—How about we go and have a look? Maybe we could find some traces of a landing.

—Then let's go now before anything gets wiped out. Take your hunting rifle and get some torches. Come on, Leopold! You have to show us where it happened.

—No, no—I am afraid. I don't want to go back there!

—We are ALL going. You have nothing to be afraid of. Come on, let's go!

—Well, guys, we will spread out like a line of beaters, and with our torches, we will comb the area.

—We can't see very well.

—Hey! There! Look over there! There is a spot where the grass has been trampled!

—Yeah, but that could mean anything.

—Do you smell a curious odor in the air?

—Yes, maybe. But it does not smell like fuel or anything else that I can remember. Bizarre, for sure.

—Mates, over there! Look at the sky! There's a bright white round thing just over the trees—the flying saucer!

—No, you idiot—that is the moon. Have you never seen the moon? Stop! Enough of this bullshit. Let's go back.

—Wait, wait! Over there, across the valley and on the next hill—can you see that curious light moving?

—When will you be finished with seeing aliens everywhere? Is this contagious or what?

—But look! There *is* a light! And it is moving! And you know that nobody lives there! What do you say it is, if you are so smart?

—I don't know, and I don't care. As far as I am concerned, the little green guys can come and go as they like and catch the rabbits and confuse them for humans. Me, I am done with this joke. Leopold gets boozed like a sponge every evening, and next time, he might just take us hunting for pink elephants. But that will happen without me. OK, guys, I'm outta here! Good night!

—OK, everybody, we better leave this matter for our usual meet at the bistrot (*1) this Sunday.

—Hey, guys, did you see the paper?

—No. What's in it?

—That bastard Leopold told his story to the local journalist, and there is an article with a picture of him. See page 2. The headline is "Has a flying saucer landed in Saint Mallard en Barrois?"

A well-known inhabitant of Saint Mallard has been the witness of a strange scene when a mysterious object, extremely luminous, landed near his field. Two creatures came out and collected samples of the local flora and wildlife before disappearing. The gendarmeries were alerted and reported that they found traces on the ground. In our picture is Monsieur Leopold Painblanc, the involuntary hero of this incident.

—This Leopold, he is really afraid of nothing—besides the aliens!

—Ha ha! The other night, he was nearly wetting his pants!

—Yeah, but nevertheless, there must have been something happening that day—something that made him so afraid. There is no smoke without fire. He might have been boozed, but he was able to stand. And there was that trampled grass and the curious smell.

—Yes, well, if you ask me, the best thing we can do is wait for these invaders to come again, and we will see. Here, give me the paper. I have not seen the rest of it.

—Good, who'd like another drink? It's my round.

—The same for me, thanks. Hang on! Look at this article in the local page of Saumur en Barrois, our neighbors:

Poachers caught red-handed! The village warden of Saumur en Barrois did a good job last Wednesday night by interrupting the activities of three poachers who were hunting illegally by night on the grounds of Saumur and the nearby villages. They were using a technique that is strictly forbidden. One of them was operating with a strong acetylene lamp with the purpose of blinding the game that his accomplices, armed with clubs, could then easily approach and stun. All our congratulations go to this valiant servant of the law, Monsieur Auguste Leveneur, who has rid us of three unwelcome invaders!

—Last Wednesday . . . last Wednesday? This tells me something, but what?

71

But Who Is Your Dad?

—Mister President, can I have a word with you?

—Certainly, my dear colleague. The meeting's breaks are just for that very purpose.

—Thank you! The matter is that I would wish to introduce a bill to Parliament, and I would like to have your advice on the matter.

—This is your job as an MP. What is your proposal?

—Well, you know that when a new law or an amendment is discussed in the House, and eventually there is a vote, the bill usually carries the name of its creator.

—This is true, and for many of our colleagues, it is a great satisfaction to see their names associated with texts and be distinguished from the anonymous mass of their peers. Very often, it is the result of long years of more or less futile or useless parliamentary efforts that are finally rewarded.

—Yes. The law I would like to propose could help make this "paternity" more accurate, like it is now for the civil registrations.

—How so? Tell me more.

—Well then, instead of having just one name, I suggest that all the MPs who voted in favor of the bill be considered as "coparents" and referred to with numbers, such as parent 1, parent 2, parent 28, parent 122, etc.!

—But, my dear friend, surely you are not really thinking of such a thing? Will our colleagues accept being deprived of their "babies" and being reorganized and replaced by numbers? You will only find a little minority of gender activists to support you.

—Then why are we doing this thing for the children? When a very large majority of the parents want to stay being referred to as father or mother, we are giving preference to a minority who refuses gender references, and this occurred without even asking everybody who is concerned!

—Ah, my dear colleague, I certainly understand your point. The active minorities are indeed a growing problem in our society. One wants to satisfy everybody, and in the end, everybody is pissed off. Democracy is not anymore the law of the number but the law of those who are screaming louder. Furthermore, the laws and the children, they are not the same things.

—So what should I do with my bill proposition?

—My friend, propose it. Propose it, and you will see the result. I am afraid that you will always find some bigmouths who will support you and enough sheep that will follow them and vote in favor of it. And while we're at it, why not start discussing again the gender of the angels in paradise? By the way, how have you named your bill for the moment?

—Well now, I have given it my name. I am a young MP, and this is my first "baby," so to speak.

72

External Squint

—Good evening. I would like to see Madame Irma.

—That's me. Good day, Monsieur! Are you coming for a consultation?

—Yes, if you can take me. I have some problems and need your help.

—What sort of problems?

—Well, all sorts of problems—sentimental problems, health problems, and professional problems. I am depressive, I cannot sleep, and everything I do seems to be jinxed. Everything is going wrong!

—I see! But, you know, all these problems are often related. It may simply be because at the moment, you are under bad astral circumstances.

—If you say so. But I would like to know more and find a way to get through this. I hope that you can help me.

—I see! But it's not going to be easy. We will probably have to use different techniques: the card reading, the tea-leaf dregs, the crystal ball, the tarot cards, the bones, the body waves, the mind reading, the astral relationships, etc., and we probably have to plan for several sessions together. But fortunately for you, I am something of an expert in all these techniques, and at the moment, I have a special package—a very good deal. You see, this is already a good start, and for once, you have some luck!

—That's one way to look at things! And if I take the package, how much does it cost?

—Let's say five hundred euros for the first six sessions. That gives you six sessions for the price of five!

—Ah, that's still a lot of money, and I suppose you want cash?

—I would prefer cash. I can take credit cards, but I don't accept checks. You can make a deposit today and pay the rest next time if you want.

—That's good. I understand. Here is a two-hundred-euro deposit. Are you doing special prices for public servants, by any chance?

—No! I am sorry. They are often more difficult cases, and I cannot afford to do that. Especially the police officers—they have too many problems!

—Oh! How did you guess that I am with the police?

—For once, I did not guess anything, but I had a glimpse of your police ID card when you opened your purse!

—Well done, you! I should have been more cautious. Ha ha! OK. Now, when can we start? Today?

—Sure, if you want. If so, we will begin with the card reading. It is usually a good way to start, and we will get a more precise idea of your situation.

—OK, I am ready. How is it done?

—Good. Take this deck of cards. Yes, you can check them. It's an ordinary deck. Now, shuffle the cards. Very good. Now cut the cards. Perfect. Put the pack back on top. Now give me the deck and watch. I am going to draw the cards one by one without exposing their faces, and when you want, you say "Stop," and I turn the card that is in my hand at that moment.

—OK. That's simple. Let's go now.

—Right. One, two, three—

—Stop!

—The queen of spades! Oh, this is not a good start!

—Why not?

—Yes! There could be in your close circle a lady who does not want any good for you. But wait for more and continue. One, two, three, four—

—Stop!

—Five of clubs! This is not very good either! Some financial problems—those never help things.

—I must admit that, that is obviously the case. Please, let's go on.

—One, two—

—Stop!

—Jack of hearts! Of course, one had to expect this.

—"Expect"? Why?

—Well, the presence of this jack of hearts near the queen of spades is eye-opening. Don't you see?

—I am afraid to guess. Is the jack attracted to the queen of spades? Possibly her lover, to say the things more crudely! Ah, the bitch! I suspected there was something cooking behind my back.

—It's only you who say that. Don't jump to conclusions. Let's go on and see first what will be coming now. One, two, three, four, five, six—

—Stop!

—King of diamonds. Well, this is something else. It may be a clue, but wait for more. One, two—

—Stop!

—Ten of spades! This card coming after the king of diamonds points toward possible professional issues in your relationships with your superiors.

—Say, your cards, they are beginning to scare me. How is it possible to see all of this with these little pieces of cardboard? Or maybe you are reading my mind? Or what?

—You know, there are things that one cannot explain. There are waves, powers, and gifts. And if you came to see me, it is somehow because you are inclined to believe in them too. Your reaction tells it. But wait, the session is not finished. Let's keep going. One, two, three—

—Stop!

—Queen of diamonds! Well, this is another piece of the puzzle.

—What? What puzzle?

—Wait! Keep going first! One, two, three, four—

—Stop!

—Seven of hearts! Now we are starting to get an explanation!

—"Explanation"? I am waiting to hear it from you. I see nothing!

—Don't be impatient. You know that everything has already been written anyways—the past, the present, and the future—so there is no need to rush.

—Yes, I know that some say that, but if everything has already been written, as you say, I would at least like to know where I can read it. That would simplify things!

—Come on, come on! That would be too easy and too dangerous if we could know everything in advance. Let's be satisfied that we can sometimes get some indications. Monsieur, you know, it's not always easy to be a fortune teller. Sometimes people get angry about what you are telling them. Sometimes you better do to disclose some information, a close family member's death, for example!

—OK, OK, but can we please go back to my queen of diamonds and my seven of hearts, if you don't mind? What do you see that is so interesting?

—I see some sort of frustrated love affair. It's as if somebody was in love with somebody else, maybe an office colleague, but was not daring enough to declare his feelings.

—Ah! Hmm . . . do you really SEE that? Well, hmm . . . good. Could we move on and use another of the techniques you mentioned?

—As you wish. Then I propose taking a little look at the crystal ball to finish this session.

—Great! Let's try that! I'm excited!

—Wait. I have to turn off the light and blacken the room. Then I have to light the ball. That's good. Now, look straight into it.

—I see nothing other than glass!

—Of course, but you have to look with your mind, not only your eyes.

—That's easy for you to say! And you, what do you see?

—Me, I see some reflections that, at the moment, are like blurred pictures. Ah, silhouettes are coming in and out of focus. Wait.

—And now?

—There is a picture starting to form. A crowd, people fighting, blows exchanged, smoke all around—does it tell you something?

—Hell! I think I know. This is very disturbing.

—Yes, but it is still quite blurry. We will probably have to wait for the next session to know more about this.

—But you are the clairvoyant. And I cannot wait to know.

—Yes, yes, but one should not rush things. You know, these phenomena are very sensitive and hard to understand. One cannot control and interpret them so easily. Be patient.

—OK, OK. I will be patient. But, even from today, I have already plenty to think about with what you have told me. This queen of spades, this jack of hearts, this queen of diamonds—I believe I recognize them.

—Maybe, but take care and be discreet. Just observe things before coming back to see me again. Let's say next Wednesday at the same time, if it suits you.

—That's fine, but before I go, I'd like to ask you a question, if it's not indiscreet.

—Certainly.

—I am wondering why you, a sightseer, wear those dark sunglasses. Surely it cannot help you with your job.

—Ha ha, you have noticed. But, in fact, yes. Look at when I take them off.

—What! But you are horribly squinting!

—Well, yes—it is called an external squint.

—But then . . . how can you—

—It is quite simple. I have one eye looking toward the past and one eye looking toward the future. In my job, this is quite practical! So there you are. Ha ha. See you next Wednesday, and until then, take care of anything flying, Monsieur Inspector!

73

Global Warming

—Hey, hurry up and take this photo!

—Wait, I have to set the timer so that we can both be in the picture. OK, it's done.

—Quick, stand beside me and behind the pennant planted in the snow. Watch. Cheese! That's it. Now we can start our descent.

—Yes, we better not waste time. Look, there is some bad weather coming from the surrounding peaks, and fog is rising from the valley. It would not be good to get caught out in the most dangerous part of the mountain.

—OK, take the lead. I will secure you. We better use a long length of rope in case of trouble. I don't like at all the look of those black clouds over there. There could be snow coming!

—Yes, we don't need that.

—Don't worry. I know the track quite well. I have my landmarks, and anyways, we can always follow the markers that we used on our way up.

—DAMN! This bloody fog is getting thicker! I can hardly see a few meters in front of me, and I am afraid that we have missed the marker. We are going to get lost!

—Keep walking. We should try to get to the glacier, and then we can orientate ourselves. It must be somewhere to the left. Anyway, we cannot stop here. We must keep going down as far as possible so long as we can still see a bit.

—SHIT! And now it is beginning to snow, and the wind is rising. This is not good at all! The fresh snow will hide the crevices. It will be like walking in the middle of a minefield. We must find a shelter and stop!

—Yes, but at least the wind has cleared the fog a bit. There! See that black shape? I remember it is a rocky outcrop and the glacier is just behind it. We have to go around it. We should be able to find a shelter over there. Between the rock and the ice, there are always clefts.

—That's good. Let's go there quickly.

—See? I told you. It forms something like a cavern in the glacier behind the rock. We will just need to cut a few ice blocks with our piolets to close the opening, and we shall have a natural igloo—just in time for us to wait until the bad weather is gone.

—HEY!

—Now what? What happened?

—THERE IS ALREADY SOMEBODY OR SOMETHING HERE!

—WHAT!

—Yes, I tell you! SOMEBODY! Quick, give me the torch that is in your bag! It is too dark! Thank you—

—FOR GOD'S SAKE, WHAT THE HELL IS THAT?

—It looks like a heap of fur or a dead animal that was caught in the ice.

—No. That is not an animal. Look, you can see a head. IT'S A HUMAN HEAD!

—Dear, you are right. It looks like some sort of mummy.

—This is incredible. This guy must have been here for ages—maybe hundreds of years!

—What do we do now?

—Well . . . we . . . nothing! I don't think he's going to mind if we stay for a while and take shelter here. After, we will see. Come on, cut some ice blocks to close the opening of the crevice a bit. Meanwhile, I will prepare us a warm drink with our cooker. And then we will rest and wait out the storm.

—Hey! Can you stop wiggling like that? Try to sleep a bit.

—I can't. I'm thinking of HIM! It feels weird to know that he is just right there. Who do you think he was?

—I don't know. Probably a hunter who fell into a crevice of the glacier. Considering that his clothes are made of animal skins, probably deer and bear, he may be a lot older than I was first thinking. It is not uncommon for people to die on a mountain, get caught in a glacier, and reappear many years later when the glacier melts.

—Yes, but this one is breaking all the records. Only the prehistoric men were dressed like that.

—It is possible that he has been stuck in this part of the glacier for a long time. This protruding rock might have stopped the normal flow of ice down into the valley. You know, he could even have rested here and been ignored for a longer time if it had not been for the global warming.

—I have the feeling that HE is observing us. After all, we are intruding on his grave. This is his place! And what if he was revived? I saw a movie where a guy came back to life after spending years frozen in ice.

—Come on, come on—that was only Hollywood. Even if he did come back to life, we could always have a drink together to celebrate the event. Ha ha! Don't worry. SLEEP!

—I will try, but I'm pretty sure that I will have nightmares.

—Hey, wake up! I can see light outside. The storm has passed. We will be able to go down, hopefully before they send a rescue party for us.

—And what of our friend? Obviously, he has had another settled night!

—He is fine where he is now and can wait a few more days. We will mark the spot so we can find our way back here more easily. We will come back with everything we need to get him out of there.

—Come on! Let's go now! Be careful of the fresh snow and put your steps in my boots' prints. We don't want to fall into a hidden crevice and stay frozen there for centuries until more lost idiots discover us!

—Wait! We forgot to take pictures. Without them, they might not believe our story.

—Good idea! Take as many as you can and from all angles.

—Hello! Do you have any news about our discovery?

—Yes. That made a fuss of all devils, especially when experts saw the pictures. They started to send calls all around the country. Some scientists have already arrived with a lot of equipment and instruments. They have asked to be taken up there as soon as possible. They want to investigate everything at the site before removing the body. They are hoping to take him back to the valley in his ice coffin and put it in a refrigerated container. They are saying that this guy could well be about five thousand years old! Can you believe it (*1)?

—So we will climb up there again with the scientists?

—Yes, tomorrow. The weather forecast is good, and we have to use the opportunity.

—They will try to work out who he was, the cause of his death, and all sorts of things! They may even try to track down his family, like it is usually done for all disappeared people! Now they use DNA.

—Well, I wish them good luck. Finding the family of a guy after five thousand years—that could take a lot of time and concern a lot of people!

—His family? After all, WE are his family, no? We and many others!
—WE? What do you mean?

—Yes, the family of this guy—it's all of mankind. It is that simple!

*1. Otzi, the Iceman, discovered in 1991 in the Alpen at an altitude over three thousand meters, is the oldest natural mummy ever found. It is believed that he lived some five thousand years ago, in the late Neolithic period, and died from blood loss after being hit by an arrow.

Postface

Yes, our world is like the branloire pérenne (*1) of Montaigne. It permanently swings between the extremes of the absurd: the comedy and the tragedy.

And we, the unwitting passengers of our planet, have no choice but to hold on as best as we can to survive, like someone clinging to the ropes of a swing, trying to avoid being ejected.

We might often want to push Pause, step down, and stop the game, but the problem is that there are always some idiots who are pushing us in one direction or another.

We cannot escape the absurd just as we cannot escape a rocking swing—without the risk of breaking our necks in the process!

So we have to cope with it and survive—survive the stupid commands, the dumb rules, the ridiculous situations, the forced beliefs, the degenerate behaviors, the suicidal sciences, the manipulated information, the useless conflicts, the artificial hierarchies, the tricky laws, and the knife of the maniac killer waiting around the corner!

This is not obvious!

It would be preferable if we could laugh about it!

Ah, if only we were able to recognize all the idiots for what they are before they become a nuisance!

That would be fun!

This was the ambition of this book!

Didier Lucien Poppe

*1. Branloire pérenne (The world is a permanent swing)—from Michel de Montaigne.

Printed in Dunstable, United Kingdom

65891166R00156